Rodger B. Moore

SCHOOLHOUSE BURNING

AUSTIN MACAULEY PUBLISHERS™
LONDON • CAMBRIDGE • NEW YORK • SHARJAH

The story, experiences, and words are the author's alone.

Ordering Information
Quantity sales: Special discounts are available on quantity purchases by corporations, associations, and others. For details, contact the publisher at the address below.

Publisher's Cataloging-in-Publication data
Moore, Rodger B.
Schoolhouse Burning

ISBN 9798889109419 (Paperback)
ISBN 9798889109402 (Hardback)
ISBN 9798889109426 (ePub e-book)

Library of Congress Control Number: 2023916856

www.austinmacauley.com/us

First Published 2024
Austin Macauley Publishers LLC
40 Wall Street, 33rd Floor, Suite 3302
New York, NY 10005
USA

mail-usa@austinmacauley.com
+1 (646) 5125767

20240319

Acknowledgements

For their endless encouragement and steadfast contributions to this work of 'Art & Behavioral Science', the author wishes to thank:

Mary Ann McDonald-Palmer & Glen Palmer
Mabel and Gertrude Collins
Atoil Smith
Hugh Douglas McDonald VI
Reva O'Neal-McDonald & Hugh Douglas McDonald VII
Bertha O'Neal-Hankins
Shirley Davis-Moles & Armand Moles
Mark Moles
Steve Moles
Lisa Moles-Doak
Lori Moles-Wallace
Patsy McDonald-Johnson & Richard Johnson
Christie Johnson-Smith
Douglas Johnson
Yoseph Geshiri, Ph.D.
Lawrence Riley, Ed.D.
Anthony Buhl, Ph.D.
Dorothy Moore, Ph.D.
Robert Mather, M.A.
Edward Gray

Rev. John Swisher
Nina Bolling, M.A., L.P.C.
Ken Thom, M.S., L.P.C.
Authorene Phillips
All the members of the Marshall Missouri Writers Guild
The Marshall Missouri Public Library staff
The Missouri State Historical Society
The Hon. John Andrews
The Hon. James T. Bellamy
Ann Covington, Chief Justice of the Missouri Supreme Court (Ret.)

Introduction

Early on in my life, the 'comings and goings' of daily events on everything from personal needs to world events were topics of just about every meal around the table; whatever happened to be pressing at the moment. My great-grandfather was elected county treasurer during the first term of FDR in 1932, so politics was a frequent concern discussed often in no uncertain terms.

The killing of President John F. Kennedy, Officer J.D. Tippet, and Mr. Lee Harvey Oswald, and the attempted murder of Texas governor John Connelly, that fateful weekend in November 1963, was one of the most traumatizing experiences in my life, and directly or indirectly shaped the career and personal decisions I would make for the rest of my life.

After telling me about the deaths of Abraham Lincoln, John Garfield, and William McKinley, Granddad said the only way something like the killings in Dallas could have happened was if it was allowed to happen, since the President was the most powerful, watched, protected, quoted and photographed/filmed person in the world. A month short of my 13th birthday, I remember thinking, "How could we stop such a thing from ever happening again?"

Naturally, I'm a 'people' person rather than 'data' or 'things' oriented, and I have chosen to take up the cause of many public affairs issues through my life's work. The writing of this book is in the hope we can make this world a better place to live and grow in. It hasn't always been easy and I have made my share of mistakes which I've paid for, but I've always tried to live by the Ten Commandments and the Golden Rule, and I hope in the end, honesty and hard work will, like Granddad said, have their own rewards.

Chapter I: **'The Welcome Stranger – A True Short Story'** (p.13), is about an experience I had early in my life.

I learned you can't always be of help to everyone, but you have to try if no one else is able to help and you know what needs to be done, regardless of how everyone else may feel. I was compelled to intervene in a dispute between two common combatants, only to receive little or no thanks for my successful efforts, while a throng of onlookers stood by and did nothing but yell and shout insults.

It is better to let those who know what needs to be done do their best, rather than 'faking it' and just hoping things will turn out alright on their own. I've also included a reframing of an old poem I once heard when I was a child that expresses a part of my aspirations and guidelines for life.

Chapter II: **'Schoolhouse Burning'** (p.19), is about a tragedy that occurred from December 1930 to January 1931 and was the basis for much anger and resentment in our society, even up to modern times. The murder of one of society's most vulnerable, innocent, and defenseless members is the activating event for the worst and most horrible wrongful death of an accused defendant in government custody in all of recorded history; worse than Lee Harvey Oswald, Jack Ruby, and Jeffrey Epstein put together.

A creative historical review of the two killings and the surrounding events at the start of the Great Depression from a forensic/clinical psychology perspective is undertaken to solve decades old 'who done it' in an attempt to ensure such a scenario is never repeated.

Chapter III: **'Strengthening the Administration of Justice'** (p.160), presents the results of two public opinion surveys and baseline observations of three jury trials. Strategies for helping the jury and court are proposed including audio-visual tape recording of the entire trial, photographic feedback, trial audit teams, and five additional recommendations. A copy of a letter from the Chief Justice of the Missouri Supreme Court regarding my recommendations is available.

Chapter IV: **'The Republic of Jerusalem'** (p.177), critiques previous attempts at world governments/forums and proposes the 'Home Rule' of Jerusalem as an independent country unto itself with continual U.N. support and involvement. U.N. resolutions that breathed life into the State of Israel were also intended to give life to a Palestinian homeland, as well as a sovereign Jerusalem under international control. The time has come for the civilized world to keep its promises and solve the age-old disputes of the Middle East.

Chapter V: **'A Case Study in Self-Hypnosis'** (p.187) is to address many internal conflicts a person experiences through the course of their life. Can age-regression in a variation of self-hypnosis/deep-sleep format provoke an 'upon arising' conscious reliving of an individual's first trauma-resolving event in their life to promote 'wellness through mindfulness'?

Thank you in advance for taking the time to read my manuscript. I hope it will be as enlightening and enjoyable for you to read, as it was for me writing it. And, after many years of great happiness in the fields of professional behavioral and mental health counseling and psychology, I would like to thank you for what only the Good Lord and I shall ever know.

Chapter I
The Welcome Stranger – A True Short Story

Before pandemics, cell phones, computers, fax machines, and the Internet took over most of our lives, there was a park in a southwestern American city where one could temporarily escape the pressure of modern life. The town surrounded by mountains and desert was an unlikely place to have a town. Once a trading post, it grew into a bustling city with plenty of fresh water, people, and parks.

The parks thrived on hot summer days. Towering live oaks and weeping willows shaded small peaks and lush green valleys. Playgrounds bound by steaming streets, they were havens of peace in a sea of locomotion.

One summer day at about noon, a young man was reading an interesting book atop a hill in a park. On a bench perched for a panoramic view of the entire park, he took for granted people picnicking, snoozing, or just playing with their children on swing-sets and teeter-totters; guitars played, crickets hummed and birds sang. Frisbees and balls of all kinds glided in the air, with many a traveler just passing thru.

Some people let their dogs run free in the park, acting as if they don't know who owns the animal until trouble strikes. Then tears well-up in their eyes like a mineral spring from the ground, with heroic deeds soon forgotten.

Suddenly there was a loud, sharp yelp stopping the music. Several quick howls echoed thru the park. Looking around, he saw two dogs in the distance. Head-to-head, stride-for-stride, it was hard to tell, fighting or playing.

One, a German Sheppard, was easily spotted tossing its head back and forth. Ivory white teeth and a distinctive large pink tongue stood out in sharp contrast to a shiny black coat. The other, an Irish Setter, had a shimmering reddish glaze reflecting from a long coat. This poor spirit was left to cope with the evils of life due to chance. Appearing to lunge like a living dagger at Sheppard's throat, the young man wondered, "Why?" Anyway, was he his brother's dog keeper?

One, then two boys converged upon the scene. No luck. One man, then another, tried to reach the dogs. The more they tried, the further away the canines struggled.

By this time, the young man was yelling, "Kick them!"; a stupid thing to say, let alone think. He had dogs growing up, knowing sometimes they just like to 'waller' around and wouldn't listen, but the comment made him feel heartless. Remembering an old Chinese proverb 'words can't cook rice', he dropped his book coming off his bench.

A group grew around, including the dogs' owners. They all shouted at each other to end the sickening madness, making the dogs more agitated. The moment of power was not to be for these city folks or kids who shouldn't put themselves at risk. A woman's voice from the crowd cried out, "Someone help!"

Now briskly walking toward the commotion, the young man made his way through the crowd like Moses parting the Red Sea. Seeing a choker collar around Sheppard's neck, the silver-on-black image sent a thunderhead cloud over him. Made of chain links, the collar and leash can strangle its captive if pulled long and hard enough. Letting go, the collar could be removed. The leash was dragging on the ground.

Sure enough, the chain had been slack enough to wrap around the lower jaw of the Setter in a 'crisscross' fashion while the rest of the chain was still in place. He felt even more startled, witnessing blood flowing from the Setter's mouth while insults from the crowd grew louder.

Kneeling by the tangled hounds, he whispered, "Not pretty." The Setters' blood was due to a missing large front tooth. One link of the chain was wedged over another tooth. Torture to endure, let alone watch, they flailed around more violently. Not an easy problem to solve without the courage to take a chance. He took it.

The first attempts resulted in more jerking and yelping. Quietly gentling the dogs in a calm but confident voice, he asked the owners to sit on their respective pets. Holding their heads close together should create enough slack in the collar.

The soft tone, understanding inflections of a quiet voice, and the gentle touch of his hands said more than words ever could. His crystal blue eyes with a forever-young face became one with the dogs in peril.

Guiding their heads together, he placed his hands on either side of the Setter's jaw. His fingers around the wedged link, lesser whimpers followed. A sudden hush fell over everyone. All at once, the birds, crickets, and time seemed to stand still.

A passerby asked, "Why is this taking so long?" Impatiently, the young man explained what he knew. The passerby said, "Go ahead, man. You got it to do."

The thought of putting fingers in the mouth of an unfamiliar bleeding dog was scary at first. Also, the Sheppard could suddenly bite at anyone getting too close. But after all, who would bite on a chain? Was the Sheppard going anywhere without help? With just enough slack in the collar, his thumbs gently felt the soft pink moist underside of the Setter's tongue. Dislodging the stuck link, relief with freedom was won.

Before the Setter blindly bolted past its owner's outstretched hands moist with tears, our hero felt a raspy lick on his fingers. He called out, "Take him to the Vet!" 'Licitly-split', the pair disappeared down a path to the sidewalks. They learned the hard way, well-intended 'rough-housing' could have its hidden dangers too. They would learn in time, it's the traumas in life that make us stronger if we remember what it took to resolve them.

The Sheppard looked up with a whimper as if to ask, "How could you leave me this way?", before licking its owner's hands and face. More passive, standing its ground, the dog was ready to go on with life. Picking up the leash without a word, the owner and dog walked away. This couple knew the flame of peace could be easily extinguished. While patience and belief in one's self are essential, always be prepared to be tested by steel.

The young man walked back to his bench to resume reading. There was no thanks from anyone except the dogs, but as he walked, he felt the calm he had enjoyed before. He learned disasters only worsen when people try to help without knowing how, and as much as you try, you can't outsmart getting hurt in life. Waiting for an invitation won't do either when you know in your heart worse disasters loom.

As the sun started down in the western sky, Frisbees flew, birds chirped, crickets hummed, guitars played and a gentle breeze carried away the memory of many a welcome stranger.

THE END OF 'THE WELCOME STRANGER'

Values and Principles – A Poem

My principles, I will not forsake,
I will keep the promises I make.
If my values, I would have to defend,
Upon my principles, I would always depend.
On honesty, I will always rely,
And lies, I would forever defy.
I would live a life above reproach,
Upon another's repute, I would not encroach.
Our values are not gauged by our worldly gain,
They are built upon principles that have not a stain.
If such an honor, I can attain,
I shall not have lived my life in vain.
These few lines to you I sing,
They tell of the life, I strive to bring.
To live the virtuous, honorable life,
Is for all, the greatest thing!

Chapter II
Schoolhouse Burning

This is a story about the ills of human nature and what can happen when a person(s) is stimulated by a 'trigger' or activating event so compelling, they will stop at virtually nothing to 'right-a-wrong' or hide the truth that threatens the security of them, their family or community.

In an attempt to restore peace, harmony, and protect themselves and their own, an individual or group will go to any and all lengths as a means of restoring the social order they feel is most safe, productive, virtuous, and honorable for the future of themselves or their group. This holds true for virtually every social group that doesn't have safeguards built into the group's system of government protecting the rights of minority members and even some who say they do.

Thus, when it seems that peace and harmony have been restored by the display of group violence toward the alleged offending individual(s), the group can mistakenly believe those actions hold the most promise for a prosperous future, discouraging anyone from repeating the actions that created the initial 'trigger'.

This is clearly a false assumption, as the 'trigger' may have been created to distract people from others, who may have actually created the 'trigger' or other crimes. The real perpetrators and motive(s) of those responsible for creating the 'trigger' to begin with, may go undiscovered and free from punishment to continue their plans for selfish gains.

The lessons I learned by virtue of completing many years of research on this story, others had tried hard to teach me when I was too young to fully understand. Over time, it seemed to be a double standard and I was always testing what should be accepted or not. It all sounded too naïve to be totally believable.

I was brought up to believe the law was for the protection of all the people, the Ten Commandments, the Golden Rule, and 'good' will always triumph over 'evil'. The truth will make you free, is its own reward and is mightier than the sword, with honesty and hard work always paying-off in the end.

Unfortunately, what they didn't tell was these standards might not apply to all people under all circumstances. The 'truth' may be just a lie that hasn't been discovered yet, and the 'end' might be when you are no longer in this world. The wind has blown away the ashes and memories of many a human sacrifice; heroes and villains alike.

This story is in the genre of creative historical mystery and forensic psychology. The publication of this story represents the fulfillment of a promise I made to my grandmother, and myself, to try and make this world a better place; learning from the mistakes of the past, and ensuring nothing like these events would ever happen again. Possibly, only an improved jurist prudence system in this country, and time, will tell whether I have truly fulfilled my promise.

The names of the actual people, places, and entities involved in the events described in this story have been changed in order to protect the innocent, of which there were very few. Disclaimers aside, the facts can't be wished away and the reality of pointless waste in all human tragedy remains to haunt us all the days of our lives. Tragedy unobserved, or remembered, is a sin of the collective conscience of our society.

This chronicle of 30 days from December 1930 to January 1931 is written in the hope insight, wisdom and a workable principle will be gained from analyzing the true events. This story is dedicated to those who will learn to recognize the potential tragedy in a seemingly harmless situation and take preemptive action to avoid it; not make the same mistakes for future generations to anguish over, and learn that criminals are like those who crawl in the low places on earth; trying to conceal their wrong-doing. They always leave trails like snails that shine in the light and eventually will reveal their presence.

The Word

Can you remember the first time you ever heard the word 'nigger'? Sadly, I can.

I was 6 years old one warm sunny Saturday morning in late August 1957, just 4 months short of my 7th birthday. I was riding with my 4-year-old brother, Mike, in the backseat of granddad's new four-door Chevrolet Bellaire sedan with granddad, proud as punch, driving; dad, stoic as always, riding shotgun.

Two-toned cream over copper in color with a fresh new car smell inside, we were traveling due southwest of the town, Berryville, County of Nowadays, USA. Mom, Aunt Pozzy, and Grandma had already started out on the eighteen-mile trip to our fried chicken dinner destination with my 3-year-old brother, Stephen.

As we slowly drove on a two-wheel dirt path through a cornfield overgrown with nine-foot-tall tasseled stalks, brown silks, and sharp green leaves brushing by endlessly on my fingers, Granddad calculated this was the best shortcut to my Great Aunt Marie and Great Uncle Gary's farm. There, they lived off the rolling hills, raising livestock, row crops, garden fresh fruits and vegetables with my great-grandfather Mickey. The kind of hills, if you went over them too fast, you could feel butterflies in your stomach coming down the other side.

As we came to a gravel crossroad, granddad said, "Up there is where they burned that nigger." Pointing to his left, he said, "Do you want to go up and see?" Dad just slightly shook his head 'no' and motioned with his hand to go on.

I jumped up on the floorboard, hanging over the front seat, straining to see what he was talking about. Only an empty gravel road disappearing straight over a small hill to our left with ripe cornfields on either side was visible. I didn't know what 'nigger' meant, but I certainly knew what 'burned' did.

I asked dad what granddad meant but he just sat quietly watching the road ahead and motioned for me to set down with my brother. For the rest of the trip, no one spoke a word. Mike and I sensed this was not a subject open for discussion. As Granddad predicted, we got there first by just a few minutes.

Getting a welcome hug from Mickey upon arrival, my brothers and I ran to the barn to see how much the milk cows' spring calves had grown, play with the kittens and their dog, Butch. During some visits, we would just wander around looking at how much had changed, or not, since our last visit, especially in the apple orchard. The house and yard surrounded by towering live-oak, elm, walnut, and weeping-willow trees was an island of shade in a sea of sunshine on the cleared hills of a hundred-twenty-acre farm.

With a variety of roses, peonies, azaleas, and just about every kind of flower you could imagine, they were able to keep the garden, house, and yard beautiful and tend all the cattle, hogs, sheep, chickens, turkeys, and crops year round. I remember thinking it must have taken a small army to keep up the place but only the three of them lived there.

Before long, Butch lead us instinctively to the garden where Aunt Marie, grandma, Pozzy, and mom were hoeing weeds and picking the last of the strawberries, watermelons, and rhubarb they would put in their skirts made into laps. When Marlene saw us boys, she stopped what she was doing, greeted us with a smiling "Hello, Boys," and two thumbs up, and told us we could help get dinner ready, starting with washing our hands and picking strawberries. She would pay a quarter for every full box we could get to the kitchen.

Finishing with the strawberries, Aunt Marie and I gathered eggs in the henhouse and I asked her what granddad had meant on the way out. She said, "That was a long time ago, before you were born. You don't need to worry about things like that. Maybe when you're a little older, you can have your granddad tell you about it. He was there."

For the rest of the day, I hounded everyone as to what a 'nigger' was. They all said I should never use that word again, ignored me, and went about their chores. Aunt Pozzy, nine years my senior on the front porch swing, finally told me it was a slang word for bad Negroes; much the same as 'Cracker or Honky' was for bad white people. Then, the reality of what had happened on that cornfield hill began to sink in.

Dad, age 28 and a Korean War 'Purple Heart' veteran, was 2 years old at the time of the incredible 'burning' incident that took place about 26 years prior. He told me once there was only one African-American man and his family that remained in Nowadays County after the incident. Dressed in gray khaki pants with a T-shirt, he was generally quiet but when he spoke, you listened. College educated, tall and muscular build, he had dark brown eyes with medium length black hair and was always clean-shaven.

He had just started developing a farmers' livestock cooperative that would provide farmers with an alternative marketplace for their produce. Whenever we started the long trip to see my grandparents, we would always wonder if he would stop along the way to see a man about some pigs, while the rest of us waited in the car.

Only judging you by what you did, he believed the only fools he ever met were the ones who opened their mouths to prove it. If you talked for more than an hour on any one given subject, you were talking more than you knew. And, if you don't work, you don't eat; handouts make beggars out of people.

Mom, age 26, (9 months in grandma's womb at the time of the 'burning' incident) was slender build and medium height with blue eyes and long light brown wavy hair, shoulder-length, usually parted in the middle and had a natural curl to it.

Always with a bold bright smile, she was a stay-at-home mom who did more than two women's work, raising us boys and trying to put dad in the strongest position to achieve his goals. She helped out at home and worked at Penny's and the Tivoli jewelry store as a clerk while completing one year of college before starting a family.

Finding plenty needing to be done to help all of us be the best we could, she believed our education was paramount, and went back to school herself after getting her children mostly raised and eventually became a school guidance counselor. She told me once she had never even seen a 'black' person until she was about 12 years old. She believed never let your emotions get the better of you.

Aunt Pozzy, age 15 (born 13 years after the burning incident) was short in stature but with buxom slender features, blue eyes and short curly brown hair. She was always looking out for us kids and would see to it we never got into too much trouble. If I was crying or pouting, she would lean over me asking, "Little bitty all right?"

In her youth, Pozzy was always skipping out the backdoor of the kitchen when it was time to wash the dishes; usually to go see her best girlfriend, who lived next door. She believed if you couldn't have a good time doing it, then why do it. A cheerleader in high school and active in just about every social group there was, she would eventually get her R.N. credentials and retire from a rural community hospital after raising two children and six grandchildren.

Granddad, age 51 (24 at the time of the 'burning'), dressed in gray khaki pants and shirt sleeves rolled up, was high-school educated, average height with a muscular build, and always clean-shaven. Dark brown eyes, greased back black hair parted in the middle with 'Brill Cream' you could smell all the way down the street, and a pencil sharpened with his pocket knife behind his ear under his carpenter's hat, he ran his own construction business.

Always about the business-at-hand, he used to take me with him around town to the different job sites he had going, pointing out all the houses he had built along the way. Whenever we met after a long absence, he would ask, "How's your 'copperosity egashuating'?" or "How's your pingderinkterum hanging?" Naturally, I didn't know what to say. Eventually, I caught on and would say, "OK. How's yours?", and he would just smile, knowing I was finally catching on.

He used to say, "If you meet a child walking down the street, give them a nickel because you just never know who you might be related to." And "You can't get a decent day's work out of a person who is starving, upset, lonely, or sleepy." And you can't expect to get paid more today for the same amount of work you did yesterday. If you want to make more, produce more. And, you can't spend money you haven't got.

To hear him tell it, he had practically built the town of my birth. With him, you worked before you played, never duck a legitimate question, and always speak your mind.

He'd say, "Watching and listening to your teachers and parents, and asking sensible questions, is how you learn".

A fabulous card player, hunter, and fisher-man, he enjoyed playing poker in his younger days. Grandma put an end to that, but not other card games. He always regretted never getting a royal flush but believed something good comes of everything if you look at it right. He would say, "To pursue honor is the greatest purpose, so hook your ladder on a star and climb to it!"

Grandma, age 46 (19 years old at the time of the 'burning' incident), was short in stature but full-figured with a medium build, light complexion, dark brown hair, and hazel-green eyes. She had quit school after junior high to go to work sewing clothes, working with her mother, Momo, and her sister, Vera, at a local cafe. Her father had passed away when she was twelve, and she met granddad and Aunt Marie when she went to work for Mickey after his wife, Callie, became ill and required in-home care.

She would eventually run a fabric/children's clothing store uptown. Seldom complaining, she spared the rod most of the time but was willing to call "a club-a-club" in pinochle, or any time she felt it was politically correct. She believed when you find a job you can work at as a career that is 'a picture of love'.

Mickey, a 76-year-old widower (49 at the time of the 'burning' incident), was medium height and stout build with receding short white hair and no teeth I could see when he smiled. Father of four, he had been a farmer with his family and county treasurer for one term during the 'Roosevelt Years'.

With a love for raising lambs, he helped build the 1904 St. Louis Worlds' Fair and fathered great aunt Marlene into the world the same year, great uncle Bill the next year, and granddad the following year. The year after that, his fourth child, Henry, didn't survive to see his first birthday. He believed true giving is only when you give off yourself, for one day, all things will have to be given up.

Mickey seemed to always be in work clothes and enjoyed taking me for a 'ride on the pony', (on the toe of his boot) when he had time to play. I always felt safe around him and everyone was always asking him what he thought, even if he did have hair growing out of his nose and ears. Within the next year, he would pass away from pancreatic cancer in his sleep at the old St. Francis hospital on E. 1st St. where I was born.

Great Uncle Gary by marriage, age 53 (26 at the time of the 'burning' incident), had been hauling hay in a nearby field since breakfast. He was always in coveralls too, except when he went to Saturday night 'Hoe-Downs' with Aunt Marie, Sunday church services, Christmas or anniversary celebrations.

He had piercing dark blue eyes, a square jaw, a stern brow, and a full head of white hair, very stout and looked like he could carry a mule on his back if he had to. He believed you can't get lard unless you boil the hog. I asked him once, "What's the key to a long and successful marriage?" he said to leave the job at work, and home at home; never mixing the two. Good deeds are love you can see.

At the time, Marie and Gary had been married for about thirty years but didn't have any children. Gary would make it to the house in plenty of time to visit with everyone and eat before returning to the fields but seemed to let Marie do most of the visiting. I think he felt like he couldn't get a word in edge-wise.

Great Aunt Marie, age 52 (25 at the time of the 'burning' incident), was of medium height and build with hazel eyes, graying long hair pinned up and a forever-young-looking face. She always seemed to be busy doing something whether it was looking after Mickey or the women's church group, fixing meals, cleaning the house, ironing, sending out greeting/thank you cards, planning the next day's agenda or just doing whatever needed to be done. She could tell a story about any experience she had had, better than anyone I ever heard in my life.

Many a night, we would set up until after midnight listening to her relate past experiences. Never making fun of anyone but herself, she could laugh in a way that made everyone listening want to laugh too, whether they got the punch line or not. A pro-social Type A personality for sure with a few generalized anxiety features you would see in just about anyone who had been raised on a farm and lived through the first half of the twentieth century in this country, she believed in 'conquer your fears and you can conquer any disaster'.

I would come to be known as Grandma's boy, Mike as Momo's boy, and Stephen was everyone's boy because of his cuteness. Three years later, I would also have twin sisters: Ann and Sue (not identical; one had red hair and one had black).

At high-noon sharp, we all sat down to a delicious bountiful meal in the dining room with a long old dining table covered with a pure white tablecloth, cloth napkins, solid silver-wear and shinning wood carved matching chairs left over from the turn of the century. Aunt Marie always sat at the end closest to the kitchen so she could get whatever was needed, while Mickey sat at the other end and all the rest of us in-between.

Besides fried chicken that seemed to melt in your mouth, the meal included piping hot mashed potatoes and cream gravy, peas, carrots, green beans, celery tomatoes, radishes, spinach, and today-baked bread with fresh churned yellow butter that filled the whole two-story house with a smell that could make a rock salivate.

On that day, Aunt Marie would top it all off with churned ice cream and apple pie straight out of the oven for dessert. I like drumsticks best, and as an added touch, we would have a big slice of chilled watermelon at about three o'clock to wet our whistles on a hot afternoon of work and play.

While we were poor by today's standards, these were my first teachers in my life, and at the time, I could find no fault with them. They instilled a value system in me that served as the basis for most everything else I would do for the rest of my life.

Anglo-Saxon, Scottish, Irish, a little French, and a touch of Native American (Grandma thought Arapahoe), as blended a family as ever there was before such a label for it ever existed, it seemed a land and life of homegrown plenty, sewn together with cloth 'from the field to the bed', and given an even chance, only limited by one's own desire to learn and grow that couldn't get any better.

I remembered wondering, if that were true, then how could anyone deserve to be 'burned' to death on top of a deserted cornfield hill just outside of the town of my birth? Could it have been an accident?

Not likely.

In Those Days

For the rest of my life, I picked up bits and pieces about the story of Thelma Fern Holster (01.19.1910 to 12.16.1930, age 20 years, 10 months, 27 days at TOD), and Reginald Gumm (01.10.1904 to 01.16.31, age 27 years, 0 months, 2 days at TOD). A nice lady at the public library was the first person I heard use these names. Atop what was now an abundant cornfield is where they both would meet their final moments on earth under some of the most horrific circumstances imaginable for both.

My investigation began taking me back to December 1930. A little over a year into what would eventually be called 'The Great Depression', ten years into a grand experiment called 'Prohibition', twelve years after the Treaty of Versailles ending World War I, eleven years before Pearl Harbor starting our involvement in World War II, and sixty-five years after Lee surrendered to Grant ending the civil war that apparently wasn't over yet (Lincoln was assassinated within a week after that).

Sunday mornings were still the most segregated hours in a week of the American experience and not just between 'blacks' and 'whites'.

There were work camps, company stores, shantytowns, and people living out of abandoned railroad cars, coal mine caves, or whatever make-shift shelter they could find, with soup lines, bread lines, and flop houses around just about every corner. In most cities, streets were filled with people pushing each other around to get what jobs or food were to be had, while notorious gang lords like Al Capone lived like kings off the profits of organizing criminal activity on a more grand scale than had ever been seen before.

Malfeasance, a graft of just about every kind, bribing officials and juries, buying votes and double voting at election time, vice/prostitution, illegal liquor, larceny, machine guns, and hand grenades had become the more often than not expected norm. 'Ax' murders in Omaha, serial child abductions/slaying, and police death squads in L.A., with 'Bonnie and Clyde' terrorizing neighbors in Texas, Kansas, Oklahoma, and Missouri, were among many other desperate acts that would be noted from this era (1929 to 1945).

Out of economic and political devastation, many a 'snake oil' salesman, including Hitler, Mussolini, and Stalin, gradually took over Europe with promises of nationalized socialism and communist manifesto cures for all that ailed the world from capitalist corruption. Basically, the same thing happened in Japan and most other parts of the not entirely civilized world.

In the U.S., anytime you didn't like the way things were going, just blame the 'Reds' or fascists, and someone would believe you. Democrats waved the banner of the common man abused by the greed of 'Big Business', while Republicans decried government regulation and intrusive control of private enterprises, making it less and less profitable to be in business at all. In hindsight, all could have been predicted with a little logic learned from history. It wasn't the first economic collapse ever recorded.

An accident waiting to happen, the indulgences of a country allowing people to speculate with money they didn't have, and leaving our neighbors to put out their own fires made it seem possible anyone could get away with just about anything.

Anyway, who cared besides the preachers on Sundays, or the Temperance League fanatics anytime they got fed up? Consuming impure fermented and distilled spirits, and soda pop made from coca plants, industries operating with no regard for environmental safeguards or worker protections, and a wavering lack of faith in our country's system of government lead to many impulsive poor choices.

Fear naturally gripped people when they had no faith in the legal system, couldn't pay the bills, had no place to call home, decent clothing, or much of anything to eat except handouts or weeds. Fear clouded judgment in many failed impulsive attempts to achieve happiness for their children, families, neighbors, country, and the world. They all drank the same water, breathed the same air, ate the same foods, valued their families' futures, reaped what they sowed and all were only human.

With everything taking on a new value in the new order of things, most folks began hoarding everything they might have sold or otherwise thrown away, thinking it might be worth something someday. With a third of the workforce out of work and thousands of transients roaming the county trying to find work, the rich and 'well-to-do' only called it a 'depression' when they started feeling the bite.

Even then, they continued to take for granted the life they had become used to, thinking they could live off the profits they had taken from the stock market over the past 15 years since the last near-total economic collapse. Resisting temptation was supposed to be the true measure of character.

After the 'Crash', October 29, 1929, brought a screeching halt to the 'roaring twenties', farmers were hit the hardest, losing homes and farms they had worked as landowners and share-croppers for generations to mortgage lenders who called their notes.

Many banks, businesses, and crop failures would create a snowball interactive devastating effect. It would seem all of life had become as unpredictable and uncontrollable as the weather. The Testaments had proclaimed the love of money as the root of all evil and somehow predicted everything that was coming to pass while a growing number of empty, abandoned grand old plantation houses and homesteads dotted the countryside.

In rural areas, some folks would fish, hunt and forage off the land to live and support families no one else cared about. Some women even dressed like men trying to get work. Among many new laws passed to heal a hemorrhaging economy, employers were prohibited from hiring women when there were qualified men available who had families to support. At times in desperation, farmers would cut down trees to allow livestock to forage on the leaves.

In reaction to the new realities of the times, others would be making up rules as they went along, and political patronage would regain a prominent role. The government said good times were just ahead, unemployment rates were certain to drop and there was nothing to be afraid of except fear itself. (It didn't make sense to me the first time I heard it, but many believed it.)

Fifteen months into the Great Depression, the collective internal judge of the God-fearing good citizens of Nowadays County went haywire. They were outraged by one of the most heinous crimes ever to occur in their history.

Reflexively, they would almost unanimously decide to set a good example of a bad example when they acted on those beliefs held so dearly; "an-eye-for-an-eye; blood-for-blood" won out. In desperation to restore peace, harmony, and justice for one of their most vulnerable members, they let their emotions override their reason when they felt the proper authorities would fail to achieve justice for all. Many sinned by silence and no one was without sin.

The Scene of the Crimes

Located in Missouri's glacial plain region, Nowadays County is a border county with Iowa and the largest of six counties in what was to be called the 'Platte Purchase of 1836'; 3,149 square miles just north of present-day Kansas City, east of the Missouri River, all the way to the Iowa border.

The U.S. government, under the auspices of William Clark, Superintendent, Bureau of Indian Affairs (of Lewis and Clark fame), paid a whopping $7500 to representatives of local Native American tribes that inhabited the region originally established as a Native American reservation (Sisson, 1911).

Made up of primarily Pottawatomie and other tribes that seasonally migrated through the territory, they were all driven to extinction or exile when 'white' settlers started legally invading the territory with their own slaves and sliced up the pie of the 'bread basket of the world'. Today, it is still the Missouri county with the largest number of acres in agricultural production, and renowned for mass-producing some of the finest swine and cattle breeds in the world.

Granddad told me once it was known as a 'bush-whacker' country during the civil war.

According to government census records, the population of Nowadays County was 27,774 in 1931. Only about 90 of those were of African-American descent, working as general laborers and farm hands, with a few rumored to be running 'speak-eases', card rooms, and houses of 'ill-repute' in the county outside of town.

On the evening of December 16, 1930, in the old Carrott Schoolhouse, about a mile southwest of the county seat, Berryville, the body of first-year teacher, Thelma Holster, was discovered after she failed to come home at her usual time. On one acre of a cleared small hilltop nearly surrounded by harvested and plowed fields, the school sat on the northeast corner where two dirt roads intersected. Roads were strewn with potholes that could break an axle, loosen your teeth or bite your tongue in two pieces if you went over them too fast.

Built in 1886, the school was a one-story, one-room plain white rectangular wooden structure, about thirty feet wide and forty feet long with a twenty-foot high center ridge pole rafter.

A large kettle stove and chimney on the north end with ten bench desks in two rows, north to south, and a small stage built at the north end where the teachers' desk was located, comprised the interior. Wooden cabinets had been built on the walls for supplies, student and teacher belongings; no phone, indoor plumbing, or electricity. Lanterns and candles would be used for periodic evening community gatherings.

With only one door facing the south, there were three windows on each of the east and west long sides of the building; two windows on the north side and no windows on the south side. There were two outbuildings: A boys/girls privy and a coal shed located on the east side of the school; a well-pump adjacent. A wood plank sidewalk leading about 40 feet from the front door south to a gate at the road was the only place to walk without getting in the mud or light snow.

With the exception of two large leafless live oaks located on the west side of the building for shade in the afternoon, there were no other trees or buildings blocking the view of the location for miles in any direction. From the southwest outskirts of town or atop the courthouse on a clear day, one could easily see the school in the distance.

Overcast clouds and light snow in the middle of December day, it was a desolate, cold, and foreboding scene greeting students scurrying to class, until you got inside. Heaven helps you if you got the next bucket of fresh drinking water or had to go to the toilet.

'Red' in the Papers

As of last count, there were about 160 articles published in local, regional, and national newspapers and magazines regarding the 'burning' incident, while only a hand full of articles, mostly in local and regional papers, were ever published about Thelma's demise. I attempted to obtain permission from numerous publishers of periodicals in existence at the time to reprint various articles in their entirety.

Most of them are no longer in existence today. Those few that are, did not respond to my numerous requests, for whatever known or unknown reason(s). I question why none of the actual reporters of the articles were ever identified by name in the periodicals. The following are paraphrased headlines and excerpts from December 17, 1930, to January 30, 1931.

Cruel Attack: Angry Posse Seeks Killer, Body of Thelma Holster, 19, in Schoolhouse, Assault Before Murder. J.P. Johns, prosecuting attorney of Nowadays County called Leroy S. Marlowe, Chief of Detective, asking for the help of St. Joe Police in the investigation. Chief Marlowe will send F.C. Dobbs, Superintendent, Bureau of Identification, and a pair of detectives to aid in the investigation.

Dec. 17. Surprised without hope that her outcries would be heard, the pretty nineteen-year-old schoolteacher, Miss Thelma Holster, was maliciously attacked and beaten to death late today in the lonely Carrott School, four miles west of here, after dismissing her pupils. News of her death spread like wildfire over the countryside with the discovery of her body a 6:30 o'clock, and an incensed population aided the sheriff in search of fields and woods of the vicinity for her slayer.

Bloodhounds picked up a trail at the doorway of the school but lost it about one hundred yards south of a culvert. The search continued until 11:30 o'clock when a halt until daylight was called. Several vagrants were detained. Threats against the young teachers' attacker were voiced in the crowd drawn to the scene. Three hundred persons were gathered at the school at one time.

Coroner J.B. Watson of Barnyard said Miss Holster had been struck repeatedly about the head and fiendishly attacked. She was covered with blood and her clothes were shredded. Sheriff Harry English said it was evident she had been beaten with a blunt instrument. No such weapon was found although the coroner said fingerprints could be clues to the girl's killer were found.

Her body was discovered by H.T. Sampson, a farmer, at whose home a mile south of the school Miss Holster had lived since the start of school in September. He had become concerned for her when she did not return after school. He went there, only to find her lifeless body just inside the door of the dark deserted building. Miss Holster had been told by the superintendent of schools not to stay in the school after dark, but she apparently had papers to grade and had worked on after class was dismissed.

Will Oldy, a farmer, who lives half a mile from the school, said while plowing near it about 5 o'clock Monday afternoon, he saw a man skulking along fences near the building. Later the man entered it after Miss Holster had gone. Oldy assumed he was a hunter.

The daughter of Mr. and Mrs. George Holster, who live some eight miles south of here in the Rockford community, was serving her first term as a teacher. She took charge of the school early in September. She graduated from high school in 1928 and attended the State Teachers College here for one year. She was active in the girls' glee club, the school chorus, the Girl Reserves, and the Commercial Club.

Led by Holmes' bloodhounds from Atlanta pushing the search, Coroner Watson directed an intensive investigation of the premises and the circumstances surrounding Miss Holster's violent death. He also selected a jury for an inquest.

UNKNOWN IMBECILE KILLS CARROTT TEACHER IN SCHOOL. THELMAN HOLSTER, 20, IS ASSAULTED AND KILLED. NO DEFINITE CLUES WERE FOUND IN THE SEARCH EXCEPT FINGERPRINTS. St Joe Detectives Aid Local Authorities; Bloodhounds Lost Trail.

Berryville, Wednesday, Dec. 17-Finding the homicidal maniac who assaulted and brutally murdered Thelma Holster, a 20-year-old schoolteacher in the Carrott School, four miles southwest of here late yesterday afternoon, continued with added urgency today. Local authorities are being assisted by St. Joe Detective, S.T. Spade, M.P. Archer, and also F.C. Dobbs, head of the Bertillon staff at St Joe in efforts to solve the most outrageous crime this county has seen in years.

Clues consist of bloody fingerprints in the school and testimony as to the lurking of a man in the vicinity on the afternoon of the crime, as well as the preceding afternoon. Bloodhounds lost the trail at about midnight. They were again put on the trail this morning. Authorities worked throughout the night calling police in other towns to be on the watch for suspicious characters. Evidence of the crime was carefully planned was offered by two boys who live in the neighborhood.

William Oldy, son of Roger Oldy, and the small son of Mr. and Mrs. A.K. Burrows, who lives in the vicinity, offered these valuable clues. William Oldy said he had seen a man on the edge of a cornfield about fifty yards from the school Monday afternoon at about 3:45 p.m. Young Oldy was plowing at the time and was about a quarter-mile away. He said the man hung around the school for an hour until Miss Holster left the school to return to the home of Mr. and Mrs. H.T. Sampson, where she was staying.

Oldy said the man then started toward the road down which Miss Holster was walking, whereupon the little teacher began to run, whether because of the cold or from fear is unknown. The little Burrows boy said he had been scared by a man who had been prowling around the school yesterday afternoon a short time before the crime was committed.

Frightened, the boy ran all the way home. Another boy also said he had seen the man and added he seemed to be wearing a duck coat and cap. Other children gave similar stories but no clue to the identity of the man was gained. Descriptions were vague.

Shortly after daylight, S.T. Holmes and his son of Atlanta put bloodhounds on the trail. As was the case last night, the dogs went south two hundred yards until they reached a small bridge. Here the scent led into the ditch alongside the road and then returned to the road. Half a mile south of the school the dogs followed the trail into a cornfield and went to the back door of a farmhouse. Going around the house, they seemed to lose the trail.

Mr. Holmes took them back to where they entered the yard, and again they went to the house's back door. They went around the house again and went east. Losing the trail, they could not be put back to it. Little significance was attached to the fact they went to this particular home.

Other attempts were made to put the dogs on the trail but the only discovery of importance was the spot where William Oldy said he saw the man waiting in the cornfield. A depression in the ground where the man had sat as well as the imprint of a rubber heel in the soil was found. Unfortunately, the dogs did not take the trail.

F.C. Dobbs of the St. Joe Bertillon Bureau arrived at 10:30 a.m. At that time, most of the activity was in the school where fingerprints were taken. Dobbs said the St. Joe detectives had orders from their chief to stay on the job until finished. At 11:30 a.m., he made a further investigation of the floor of the school for fingerprints. He had not secured the purported sheet of paper said to have a fingerprint on it, which was in the hands of Dr. J.B. Watson, Coroner.

National Guardsmen were still at their posts at 12:30. Two men picked up at Bedford this morning were released after questioning by the prosecuting attorney. Other unknown men in town were detained by the police last night. Five hundred men went to the scene of the crime early last night when the news reached town. At 9:00 p.m., Mr. Holmes came with the bloodhounds. Mr. Holmes and Clum Roote went into the school with Prosecutor-elect Virgil Sternwood and Dr. J.B. Watson. Much time was used in the assessment of the body and there were complaints from the crowd.

When the men came out, the mutterings grew louder and several men shouted criticisms of the way things were being conducted. Sheriff Harry English announced the hounds were going to take up the trail immediately. They ran a few paces west of the school and turned south to the cave located southwest of the building and continued south through the crowd. Police stopped the crowd from following. Not wanting to pass up some valuable clues in the dark, the decision to postpone the effort to trail the criminal was made.

Funeral service will be held at 1 p.m. tomorrow afternoon at the First Methodist Church, conducted by the Rev. Edward I. La Rose. The body will lie in the state at the church from 11 a.m. to 1 p.m. Burial will be in the Clearmont cemetery. Thelma went to high school here, although her folks live in the country.

She was a member of the Girl's Glee Club, the Chorus, the Gils Reserves, and the Commercial Club of the high school. She then went to college, getting about thirty hours of credits in preparation for teaching at the Carrott School, which is the community center of the vicinity and where may a box and pie social have been held, and where programs often are given. A peculiar incident arises in the girl's death, her parents remembered. Thelma was the same age as her brother Floyd when he died.

THE ACTIONS OF OFFICERS POINT TO A SOLUTION

Authorities refuse to make statement of progress in search for Sadistic Slayer Dec. 17. Slim and contradictory clues led police officers through Nowadays County today in search of the sadistic slayer of pretty Miss Thelma Holster, nineteen-year-old Carrott Schoolteacher.

Tonight authorities believe they have uncovered tangible evidence that may lead to an arrest. Authorities themselves refused to say whatever evidence they found that would point to the murderer, but the secrecy with which they guarded their movement and the persistency with which they followed various clues may mean their grim and thorough investigation will disclose the slayer.

Since morning, J.P. Johns, Nowadays County prosecuting attorney, has made the search with the help of three St. Joe police officers: Det. S.T. Spade, M. Archer, and F.C. Dobbs, of the identification bureau. Two men, whose names were not disclosed, were questioned late tonight.

Several people were questioned during the day, but most of these were friends of the schoolteacher, farmers living in the community, and pupils attending the Carrot School. Efforts were directed to determine if any in the area passed near the schoolhouse at or near the time of the killing. Submitted leads were followed and scant evidence obtained was put together for a genuine clew to result.

The crime perpetrated by a vagrant was well dissipated because the school is not located on a well-traveled highway, but on a side road a few miles west of here.

Students of the school saw, on two different days, a man in hunting garb prowling about the school. Statements by pupils were corroborated by Billy Oldy, a young farmer, whose land adjoins the school property. Oldy, plowing in a field about a quarter-mile from the school last Monday afternoon, told police he saw a man in a clump of trees nearby.

When Miss Holster left, the man followed her down the road. The small son of MR. and Mrs. A.D. Burrows declared he saw a man near the school the afternoon of the crime and he was so frightened he ran home. Two other pupils related the same story, except in more detail.

Authorities believe the murderer was someone who knew Miss Holster well. They point out in support of this theory any stranger in the community would quickly have been spotted since the murderer's clothes are known to have been soaked with blood. They also declare since the murderer apparently had no car in which to escape, he must be somewhere in the neighborhood of the crime. He would need food and shelter of some type.

The theory of the murder may have been committed by a former sweetheart of Miss Holster also was checked by authorities. According to police investigations, Miss Holster seldom had 'dates', and men in general held little appeal for her. Up until a year ago, it was learned, she did keep company with two different young men at the same time. She quit the company of both, and according to Mr. and Mrs. H.T. Sampson, with whom she made her home, had made only one 'date' since.

The case has been baffling from the start. Because the crime was so fiendish, police are loath to credit the murderer with the intelligence necessary to plan a 'perfect crime'. At first, there appeared to be no clues whatever. No one saw Miss Holster's killer enter the school or saw him leave. Nor could any weapon be found which the slaying could have been committed with.

An examination of articles in the room for fingerprints made this morning by F.C. Dobbs, a Bertillon expert, found none. He dusted the drawers of Miss Holster's desk but these powders did not reveal fingerprints. Many desks in the room were treated with the same results. All objects that might have been touched by the murderer's hands were examined. Likewise, a powerful magnifying glass applied to the bloodstained floor did not reveal fingerprints either.

Some believe Dr. J.B. Watson, Coroner, preserved a piece of bloodstained paper on which there was a fingerprint. Dobbs made efforts to get possession of the paper, but it could not be determined tonight whether or not he had been successful. A peculiar circumstance noted by all authorities was that there were no bloodstains on the knob of the door, which must have been closed by the slayer. Nor were there any fingerprints.

Bloodhounds brought to the scene Tuesday night soon after the murder was discovered at about 6:30 p.m. by Mr. Sampson who went to the school to see why Miss Holster had not returned home, quickly picked up a scent and followed a trail southward to a culvert. At the culvert, the bloodhounds insisted on turning off the road into a gully. Because of the darkness and the weedy growth in the ditch, the hounds were not allowed to follow the trail further. The search, then, was abandoned for the night.

At daylight, the hounds were on the trail again. In fact, several trails led to nearby farmhouses. Occupants were questioned by police. Eventually, the bloodhounds began to wander about and apparently experienced so much difficulty in following a scent the hunt was called off. Attempts were made to bring hounds from Albania, M.O., and Beatrix, Neb., but later it was decided such a procedure would bring nothing tangible in the way of evidence.

First reports of the murder to the effect Miss Holster apparently had put up a terrific struggle against her attacker were discounted upon a close examination of the interior of the school. It appears Miss Holster had no time to struggle. She was felled by one blow of some sort of metal instrument. There were five major wounds on the head, according to the coroner. He said any one of these wounds was sufficient to have caused death.

In addition to the five fractures of the skull, the coroner said, in reconstructing the crime, "Miss Holster was apparently preparing to leave the building. She had just finished sweeping the floor. Evidence of this is seen in the fresh stains of a sweeping compound on the floor.

"The fire in the large heating stove had been banked for the night and was undisturbed when I looked into the stove. An empty coal bucket was near the body of Miss Holster which makes it appear she was just leaving to bring in a full bucket of coal for use the next morning when she would have prepared for the opening session.

"Apparently, she was surprised by the murderer, who thrust the door open and quickly struck her on the head, knocking her unconscious onto a desk. After telling her, the murderer struck her four more heavy blows on the head, each producing a fracture. Persons who viewed the body before it was removed to an undertaking establishment said it was in the center of the floor near the door.

"The body was mutilated with a large knife and her clothing was torn away. Two large pools of blood spread across the floor." The coroner expressed the opinion the weapon used in the murder was a round metal object of some length and about the thickness of a man's finger. He said a pistol barrel might have been used, but he was inclined to believe the handle of a motorcar jack was the weapon.

In the opinion of the coroner, the murder was committed at about 5 p.m. Tuesday afternoon. He based his opinion on observations made three hours later. Blood clots already had formed on the floor, although the pools of blood were large ones, and rigor mortis (a stiffening of the muscles after death) also had set in, especially in the limbs. From the crowd attracted to the scene, the coroner picked a jury to view the body. The jury was comprised of C.L. Forman, F.W. Selvate, F.E. Haggerty, Ray White, Ben Hardly, and H. Traven.

The inquest will be held at a later date. The schoolroom scene of this morning contrasted sharply with what it must have been like Tuesday morning when school was in session. No hint of the tragedy to come was apparent. There were five pupils enrolled at the school and their names, followed by a row of gold stars, appeared on cardboard hanging on the wall. Anticipation of a Christmas celebration in the yuletide decorations strung about the room was noted.

From the center of the ceiling hung a large red and green paper bell with strands of twisted green and red paper swinging out of every corner. Each window shade had a Santa Claus with red and green strands for drapes. On the blackboard, there were drawings of this sleigh and prancing reindeer, Three Wise Men astride their camels swinging toward Bethlehem. Three wise owls were somberly gazing across the room. Behind Miss Holster's desk was a huge holly wreath with the words, 'Merry Christmas'.

HUNDREDS RUSH TO SCHOOL WHERE GIRL WAS SLAIN

Dec. 17. MURDER. Terrifying words passed from mouth to mouth and over the telephones shortly after 7 p.m. last night. The news of being a schoolteacher had been slain. Quickly, crowds formed downtown. The police alarm rang. Then hundreds of automobiles hurried out west of town to the Carrott School.

On a lonely corner, where two roads cross, stood a one-room school on the northwest corner. The sheriff and deputies were gathered on the corner, keeping crowds at by until the coroner came. The building faces the south on hill terrain with the vicinity dotted with trees and a large tree immediately to the west, the big limbs extending over the school. Thelma Holster, age 20 years, was in her first year of teaching.

About forty-four years ago, the district was too large and a school was built on what was then the land of W.T. Carrott. He later was mayor and city manager. The present white schoolhouse was named after Carrott and has been so ever since. The first teacher was S.G. Maude, Mayor Carrott stated. Miss Holster was a graduate of Berryville High School, Class of 1928, and later attended the State Teachers College here. She began her career as a teacher and was conscientious in her duties; often staying after the pupils had left to get work prepared for the next day.

In fact, in answer to a question she made of L.G. Sapp, Superintendent of Schools, about staying in the school after dark, Miss Holster was advised to leave as early as possible.

YOUNG WOMAN HAS FOUGHT WITH IMBECILE; INTERIOR OF SCHOOL GIVES EVIDENCE OF STRUGGLE, NO WEAPON FOUND; THELMA HOSTER, 20, WAS BEATEN AND SLASHED. MOST REVOLTING CRIME IN COUNTY HISTORY.

Berryville, Dec. 17. No school today at the little Carrott School, four miles southwest of here. The pupils and patrons were mourning the death of Miss Thelma Holster, age 20, who met her death in one of the worst crimes of Nowadays County since the Ova Hubbell family was killed twenty years ago this month by Hex Roscoe, who paid the penalty on the gallows.

Beaten and attacked by a moron in her school after pupils had gone home yesterday afternoon, the daughter of Mr. and Mrs. George Holster of the Rockford community was slashed, apparently with a knife and her body was mutilated. Thelma did not return to supper at the home of Mr. and Mrs. Sampson, with whom she lived about a mile south of the school. Mr. Sampson, taking a lantern with him, discovered the body at the school, lying in a pool of blood.

He quickly returned to his home, informed Paul Wings of the Electric Light Company, a son-in-law, who informed the sheriff. Mr. Wings and Sheriff Harry English arrived at the scene shortly after 7 p.m. last night. Dr. J.B. Watson, Coroner of Barnyard, immediately was summoned and took command of the situation, delaying until the Holmes bloodhounds arrived. Coroners' jury called at about 10:30 p.m., jury viewed the body and was then adjourned, subject to the call of Dr. Watson, which probably won't be before Thursday or Friday.

At that time, no witnesses were examined. Dr. Watson said Miss Holster was attacked and suffered various head trauma. It was apparent the assailant had beaten the girl's head with a blunt instrument, causing five separate fractures in the girl's head. Also, Dr. Watson suggested the assailant had used a sharp knife, as there were gases on the girl's face. Her nose and cheekbone were also broken.

There was a bruise on a knuckle on her right hand, indicating the girl had put up a fight. Desks in the school were displaced as the girl struggled desperately for her life. He found no signs of a weapon in or around the school.

National Guardsmen of Battery No. 128th Field Artillery, Missouri National Guard are assisting officers in directing traffic at the Carrott School where Miss Holster was murdered yesterday. They were not called out by the governor. These men voluntarily offered to assist in any way, in an effort to trace the man who committed the horrible crime.

The officers said they were glad to help in directing the heavy traffic, which is made up largely of curiosity seekers. The St. Joe police are cooperating in trailing the murderer.

Unless the murderer is captured earlier, the men of the St. Joe police have been ordered to stay here for the rest of the week. The sheriff called eleven guardsmen to act as guards. Two were stationed on each road leading to the school. Two were left at the schoolhouse. All were deputized by the sheriff.

While in college, Miss Holster was a member of the Y.W.C.A. and a student in good standing. As a student in high school, she was especially interested in the commercial department under Miss Mabel Patron. She was one of the students representing the school in the commercial section of the annual state contests. She was popular with her classmates.

Authorities working on the case request hunters who were in the area of the Carrott School at the time of the crime to come forward and make themselves known, so they may help in solving the case.

MILITIA JOINS IN SEARCH; NO CLUE IN BRUTAL KILLING OF TEACHER IN NOWADAYS COUNTY SCHOOL. Nude Body Mutilated, Miss Thelma Holster Victim of Criminal Attack Dismissed Pupils Yesterday Afternoon, Officers Think Fiend Planned His Assault in Advance, Bloodhounds in Futile Chase, Several Characters Arrested But No Evidence Against Any of Them.

Berryville, M.O. Dec. 17-'Merry Christmas' read the inscription which Thelma Holster, schoolteacher at the Carrott School, three miles south of here printed on the blackboard across the front of the room last evening. But there will be no Merry Christmas at the little school. Miss

Holster, 19, lies dead, the victim of the most fiendish murder in years.

Piecing information together, she died from a blow to the head. The nude body of the girl was found at about 6:30 p.m. H.T. Sampson, who lives a short distance south of the school, went to the building when she failed to arrive home. Dr. J.B. Watson, Barnyard, M.O., Nowadays County Coroner said the girl was the victim of a criminal attack. The killer also mutilated the victim with a knife.

Absence of the lethal weapon was puzzling the officers today who also admitted they were without a clue. F.C. Dobbs, the Bertillon expert, found no fingerprints. He planned to examine a print said to be in the possession of the coroner that had been made on writing paper.

From meager bits of information, officers came to the conclusion the killer planned the act in advance and had been watching this victim for a day or more. A farm hand who was plowing in a field near the schoolhouse reported on Monday evening he had seen a man standing near a large cottonwood tree watching the schoolteacher as she walked home. As she approached him, the man stepped behind a cottonwood tree. Apparently, the teacher became aware of the fact she was being watched and started to run toward Sampson's place.

After she had passed, the man stepped from behind the tree and left toward the schoolhouse. Sheriff English and others went to the spot pointed out by the farm hand, finding the print of a rubber heel in the mud. This print forms one of the few clues. Reconstructing the crime this morning, the officers said the teacher had dismissed her five pupils at about 3:45 p.m., staying a short time to grade papers. She made some decorations on the blackboard, swept the room, and banked the fire for the night.

With a coal bucket in hand, the teacher then started for the door, intending to bring in fuel for the following morning. As she stepped toward the door, she was confronted by the man whom she had seen watching her the previous evening. There was no struggle. The fiend apparently had made up his mind to kill his victim outright. She was struck over the head with a small blunt weapon and fell against a seat. The killer dragged his victim a few feet, where she was found by Mr. Sampson. The killer must have been covered with blood, the officers declared.

Farmland in the vicinity of the schoolhouse was combed for bloody garments the killer might have discarded. There is a possibility the slayer escaped in a motorcar but the general opinion is he fled through the fields. Bloodhounds were used last night and this morning in an effort to trail the slayer but were unsuccessful. National Guardsmen and farmers searched for the instrument of death but found nothing.

The schoolyard is scattered with iron and wood from discarded seats. The killer would have had no difficulty in finding such an instrument. Several men were arrested after the murder and are being held for questioning, although there is no evidence against any. All strange characters were checked. A posse was formed last night and scoured the countryside in a desperate search.

National Guardsmen today are watching all roads in the area of the school. An effort is being made to keep crowds away from the building. The complete absence of fingers and footprints was a mystery to the officers. The body was lying in a pool of blood and there was a plain smear where the body had been moved. Not a sign was seen of the killer who had apparently aimed at the death of his victim and made no effort to treat her wounds.

Aroused by the murder, threats of violence were heard in case there was an arrest. Chief of Detective Leroy S. Marlow sent three detectives of the St Joe Police Department to the scene last night. Popular subscriptions were being taken up today to raise a fund of $500.00 reward for the apprehension of the killer.

FIEND AWAITS A CHANCE TO ATTACK THE TEACHER. A CLUE TO MURDER IN MUDDY FOOTPRINTS; BLOODHOUNDS ARE BAFFLED BY THE TRAIL.

Berryville, M.O. Dec. 17-The madman who killed Miss Thelma Holster in a country school stalked her as a beast might stalk their prey. In the tall grass and concealment of a group of trees a hundred yards from the Carrott School, he spent hours in the biting cold awaiting an opportunity. His actions are seen in various ways. William Oldy, plowing nearby, saw him watch the school Monday afternoon and saw him hide behind a tree.

Seeing a person leave the concealment of the trees when the teacher had passed to go toward the schoolhouse, he saw the teacher running home as possibly frightened or just cold from the weather.

Yesterday afternoon, three pupils in the school saw the man again. He was creeping along in a gully near the school in such a manner the youngest of the three became afraid. They didn't go home by their usual route because they were afraid to be near the man but took a longer one. One of them ran all the way home. So menacing was the manner of the man creeping toward the school, he told his parents what he had seen.

The parents told J.P. Johns, Prosecutor, and St. Joe detectives who are working with him. A muddy record of the trail left by the culprit in the mud of the gully just where the boys had seen him was followed. In the mud are the footprints. Beneath the tree, where Oldy saw the fiend the day before the murder, are marks on the frozen earth. There is a footprint in the frozen mud.

Taking out his pocket knife, the sheriff lifted the footprint from the ground. It is being kept frozen in an ice pack as a strong link to the crime. A graphic story is told of just what happened in the condition of the little one-room school.

Miss Holster, teaching her first year, had been telling the five children who attended the school the story of Christmas. She had hung paper bells and bright streamers from the ceiling. Around the border of the blackboard, she had a pictorial story of wise men and a shining star. In the center of the blackboard, just behind her desk on which she had left books piled neatly, she had drawn a wreath with coloring pencils. It said 'Merry Christmas' to all who entered; a tragic Merry Christmas today.

Each night after school, she swept the floor and banked the fire in the iron furnace in the left corner of the room. Then she would go to the coal shed and fill the bucket. Tuesday, after school, she swept the floor, banked the fire, leaving a bit of fine coal in the bottom of the scuttle. She took the scuttle in her hand and started to the coal shed.

When found, the position of the body and the marks on the desks and floor tell the rest of the story.

A man was there when Miss Holster opened the door. It isn't known whether she recognized him. It was quite evident she set down the coal scuttle because it was beside the door, right side up. The man must have rushed toward Miss Holster and she must have struck at him because her small knuckles were bruised. The man then must have hit her with his fist, probably his left because her right eye was black.

There was an abrasion above it and her nose was broken. That blow, judging from its effect as shown by post-mortem, was strong enough to make her unconscious. He threw her against desks that were found out of line near the door. With a weapon about the width and shape of a motorcar jack handle, he struck her on the head. With four blows, he shattered her skull.

Not content with that, the man dragged the body into the aisle. With a knife, he inflicted three long, deep cuts back of her ear. Then he stripped the body, tearing most of the clothing to shreds, and attacked the girl, slashing her body in other places with a knife. The killer, according to the trail followed by bloodhounds, went to the right as he left the school, seeking the protection of an outside basement and a big tree.

He took the road, went down it about 200 yards to a bridge, then entered a gully. He stayed in the gully for about thirty yards. Then he returned to the road again at length passing through a wooden gate into a cornfield and on across the cornfield to another gate, then to the front door of a farmer's home. He evidently tried the door of the farmer's house, possibly seeking a change of clothes. Then he went around that farmer's home and to another farmer's house through all the outhouses and at last to a pigpen.

Although taken over the trail several times, hounds always lost the scent at the pigpen. The County Superintendent of Schools had warned Miss Holster against staying late at her isolated station. He has given the same warning to all other teachers in rural schools. It's known the last of the children left the school a few minutes after 4 p.m. A witness has been found who saw the door of the school open at 4:30 p.m. Was Miss Holster dead then, because the day was bitterly cold?

The National Guard stood guard all day on all roads leading to the school and permitted no persons other than authorities to go near it. The guardsmen build log fires in the road and warmed themselves in the long cold watch. Every farmer was a detective today. Everyone searched for traces of the murder weapon, which has not been found. Hundreds of persons massed at the militia barriers asking, "Is there any news?"

Efforts of F.C. Dobbs, head of the bureau of identification of the St. Joe police department, to find fingerprints in the building were unfruitful. He found smudges, but that was all. The St. Joe Dept. has assigned S.T. Spade, M Archer, and F.C. Dobbs to assist in the solution of the mystery.

Citizens quickly spread out one of the most complete nets in history as soon as the murder was learned. Militiamen were on guard. Surrounding towns and the special agents of all railroads were alerted. Radio broadcasts were made. One leader in the net was J.W. Welches, a well-known merchant, banker, and politician.

Citizens were collecting in large groups on the streets, discussing the murder. A reward fund of over $500.00 for information leading to the arrest and conviction of the killer has been raised. It was learned a brother's statement Miss Holster did not have suitors was in error. Her best girl friend said two years ago she was keeping steady company with two young men at the same time. There has been no report of any hard feelings over that and she is known to have broken off relations with both a year ago. Since that time, she has infrequently been seen with men.

The Carrott School, once nationally famous, remained closed today. It was not known when it would be reopened. Until recent years, the school was operated under the auspices of the State Teachers College as a model rural school. Educators from all over the U.S. visited it for ideas. It was the subject of numerous papers in educational publications by educators and feature articles in magazines of national circulation.

Officials have abandoned the idea that the crime was committed by some tramp. It appears to have been planned rather than an impulsive crime. Miss Holster had a good record in the college here, which she attended one year. She had high ratings in all her subjects and was a member of numerous social, educational, and commercial groups.

Funeral services for her will be at the First Methodist Episcopal Church and 1:00 p.m. tomorrow. The Rev E.I. LaRose will be in charge of the services. Burial will be in Clear Mount where the family formerly lived. W.S. Jobe related today that death occurred about thirty-five years ago at the Carrott School. Mr. Jobe was on the coroner's jury.

He remembered two schoolmates were sitting on the steps at the front of the school. It was just after Christmas and one boy was peeling an apple with a new knife he was given for Christmas. Without closing the blade, the put the knife in his left hand, and with the core of the apple in his right hand, he whirled to throw the core away, striking the other boy and piercing his heart, causing death with the knife in his left hand. The jury rendered a verdict of accidental death. In the absence of the coroner, the inquest was conducted by the justice of the peace, D.O. Ainess.

Discovery of a bloody suit of a man's underwear along a side road a mile and a half northwest of Conception is the latest bit of potential evidence in the murder case. The bloodstained garment was found by three boys: Melvin Case, John Dear, and Ambrose Collins while out hunting yesterday afternoon. They became frightened and brought it to Gabe Percell, an officer at Conception, who brought the underwear to the prosecutor today.

A rumor has been circulated that Robert Burrows has been arrested in the case. The authorities say he was not connected with the case. Investigators continued their grim effort to fit a score of minor bits of evidence into a comprehensive pattern which will lead to the arrest of the brutal moron who killed Thelma Holster in the school four miles southwest of her Tuesday. Hunters were questioned because the knife used by the madman must have been very heavy and sharp, as a trapper knife might be expected to be.

Evidence offered by several boys may play an important part in the solution of the crime. A chronological chart detailing events in the neighborhood from 4:00 p.m., when the school was dismissed, until shortly after 6 p.m. when the mutilated body was found just inside the doorway, has been drawn up by the prosecuting attorney, P.R. Johns, Jr.

An additional element of mystery was injected into the case by evidence offered by those who had been in the area of the school during and after the time the murderous assault was committed. Mr. John's chart shows after the school was dismissed, three pupils, J.W. Pinderton, Milton Burrows, and a boy named Hankens, walked east down the road.

Looking back, they saw a man coming south along a fence which runs north and south about a quarter-mile east of the school. This man crossed the road over which the boys had walked when they were about 100-150 yards away. The boys saw him go about 100 yards into the field on the south side of the road, and then abruptly to the west. The time of this incident was set at 4:15 p.m.

At 4:40, Fred Stanton picked up Jim Coburn and Earl Frazier, two boys who were trapped in the area, and let them out of this car at the same point the three pupils had seen the man emerge from the field and cross the road. The boys went to their trap line northeast of the school and turned south. He said the schoolhouse door was closed at the time. At 4:40, Harry and Ray Barber came by the school but saw nothing unusual. They were unable to say whether or not the door was open.

At 5 p.m., Robert Burrows was in a field south of the school to drive cows in a barn. Some of the cows had strayed to within 180 yards of the school, and young Burrows went around them to drive them south. The door of the school was open at that time. At about 6:15 p.m., when H.T. Sampson came to the school, the door was closed.

Could the murder have been committed at the very moment Stanton or Barbers were going by? Was the madman watching through the broken panel of the door for a chance to escape? Did he rush out after the Barbers passed only to return later to close the door he had left open?

These are some of the questions being asked as authorities continue with fitting their small bits of evidence together. No major conclusive clues are revealed. Exhaustive searching did not reveal any fingerprints at the scene. Whether by cunning or by sheer accident, the madman who stalked the girl several days before committing this outrageous crime left no trace which has been made public.

Donations of the $500 reward being raised for the person furnishing information which will lead to the arrest and conviction of the murderer of Miss Thelma Holster, are being received at this newspaper office. One check for $50 was received last night. The Baker School gave the first $5. Since the atrocious murder, a shadow has spread over the county, reaching every school and home in Nowadays County.

There is still a horror that the fiend, who so outrageously mutilated the 20-year-old teacher and left her body lying in a pool of blood in the one-room school southwest of here, may still be in the county. Women who never before locked their doors at night are seeing that every window and door is fastened. Reports of the tragedy have led people to keep their lights on all night. If the killer was in the area, the lights would tend to keep him away.

Teachers in the county quickly learned of the tragedy and left their school buildings as soon as school was over yesterday. Teachers have informed their students that they would not be at the schoolhouse in the mornings until 8:30 a.m. In the area of the Carrott School, there is constant fear the murderer may return. People in the vicinity do not know a single thing that would throw any light on the happenings in the school.

While funeral services were being held this afternoon for Miss Holster, authorities were pushing the investigation with excessive determination in an effort to trace the maniacal-minded slayer who has baffled every effort of the Nowadays County authorities and St. Joe police. Miss Holster is survived by Mr. and Mrs. George Holster, parents, a brother, Orville, Barnard, Rt. 2, and a sister, Mrs. Enis Peters, Pickering, Rt. 2. Burial is to be made a Clermont, near where Miss Holster was born.

The body of the teacher lay in state, 11 a.m. to 1 p.m. in the First M.E. Church. Curiosity seekers and friends of the slain teacher filed past her by the hundred. Around her white coffin was a mass of flowers. Over the coffin was stretched a white cloth, not quite transparent, which cut out from view any of the wounds that might have shown on the teacher's face.

The services were conducted by Dr. E.I. LaRose, the pastor. The church was filled to capacity before the services began, the balcony as well as the lower pews being filled when services began. Miss Holster was so quiet and shy in her actions, it hardly seemed possible such an end had come to her. Only a very few times has she been in the company of male acquaintances. She was not one to push herself on anyone.

Often times while she was attending high school and college here, Miss Holster would come to the newspaper office after the paper. She was always calm and never forced herself to the desk to get the daily paper. Her parents moved here from a farm and for about two years went to farming again. The mixed quartet of Kenny Checkers, Mrs. Bess T. Grout, Mrs. W.J. McMurtrae, and H.N. Hines singing 'Beautiful Isle of Somewhere' began the services.

Dr. LaRose recited the first few verses from the XIVth Chapter of St. John, 'Let Not Your Heart Be Troubled'. The Rev. T. Graham made a few comments about Miss Holster and ended with a prayer. The pallbearers were: Donald Whine, Leland Stout, Robert Coule, Leonard Burpee, Donald Stream, and Raymond O'Henry, all young men of the Rockford community.

OFFICERS MOVE SLAYER TO ST. JOE; CITY UNAWARE OF ADMISSION; REGGIE GUMM IS WHISKED AWAY TO ANOTHER JAIL.

St. Joe, M.O. Dec 19, 1930. Reggie Gumm, Negro, 26 years old, confessed last night to the murder of Miss Thelma Holster, a pretty 19-year-old schoolteacher. St. Joe police detectives hurried Gumm out and brought him to Central Police Station here.

The confession was made at midnight and citizens did not know Gumm had confessed to the most brutal murder Nowadays County has ever known. The confession came after a day of relentless grilling and numerous rumors abounding. Gumm was arrested yesterday morning by L.E. Etherton, a city officer.

Gumm had on garments with blood on them, which he said was the blood of rabbits. He pleaded for hours he was innocent but when confronted with a hell print found in mud near the school and shown it matched the heel of one of the shoes he was wearing, he admitted to the crime. Responsibility for the solution to the murder was given by Nowadays County authorities to St. Joe police detectives, F.C. Dobbs, S.T. Spade, M. Archer, a reporter who kept the heel print in a refrigerator, and J.B. Watson, Coroner, who led a large part of the investigation.

Gumm was brought before the prosecuting attorney, J.P. Johns, who spent all of Tuesday, the day after the murder, making an investigation of the residents of the neighborhood. The day's questioning revealed several persons who probably passed the building while the murderer was inside.

ADMITTED SLAYER TO STAY HERE; REGGIE GUMM, 30-YEAR-OLD NEGRO IN DANGER IF HE SHOULD BE TRANSFERRED; ONLY CONSOLING THOUGHT WITH FAMILY IS THELMA HOLSTER WAS KILLED BEFORE CRIMINAL ASSAULT WAS MADE; NEGRO HAD SERVED PRISON TIME.

St. Joe, M.O. Dec 19. The fiendish murder of a pretty 19-year-old, Thelma Holster, a teacher, has been solved with dramatic swiftness. Yesterday morning authorities admitted they did not have a lead worth following in an ordinary case. Leads were so scarce in the case every possibility was being looked into. Reggie Gumm, a 30-year-old Negro, was spirited away to St. Joe at 9:45 p.m. after admitting to the brutal killing.

Gumm's safety, if allowed to remain in Berryville after the confession had become known, was in jeopardy. The Negro will be kept in St. Joe, except for his arraignment, until the time of his trial in the Nowadays County Circuit Court, probably early in January. Officers frankly admit his life is in danger and the law to take its course demands a criminal, no matter how atrocious the crime, must be protected against mob violence.

Gumm's confession made to officials contains references to cruelty and brutality seldom equaled, according to the men who worked on the case. Only one firm consolation remains for the bereaved family; the girl was already dead when the criminal attack took place. The confession included how the girl, mortally wounded from a blow to the skull, begged her assailant for a drink of water as she lay on the floor of the schoolroom after an unsuccessful effort to protect herself with a broom. His answer to her pleas was a blow to her head.

The suspect was taken into custody yesterday morning, along with several others, when the officers thought he might possibly throw a little light on the case. A farmer remembered having seen Gumm in the neighborhood on the day of the murder. The Negro had bloodstains on his coat when arrested. He had been previously convicted of an attempted assault on a white girl in 1925. He was taken into the counsel room of J.P. Johns at 12:30 p.m.

Two hours later, it became obvious officers were showing more interest in Gumm than in any of the others who had been questioned. At 3:15 p.m., a stenographer was called. Although officers took pains to guard the identity of the man being questioned, his name was known on the streets by the middle of the afternoon. A correspondent of the newspaper sensed what the questioning and the calling of a stenographer meant. A late edition announced important developments were at hand.

Although not identifying the prisoner by name, the story declared that he had been convicted previously of a crime of violence. Gumm used to frequently questioning the officers on many charges, which was naturally a problem. He was known as a tight-lipped man and the officers didn't believe they would be able to secure an admission from him. Previously serving about 4 years of a 5-year term for an attempted assault on a co-ed at the State Teachers College, being sentenced in 1925, he served enough of the time to be released last year. He had also been in trouble at Omaha.

At present, a charge of carrying a concealed weapon is pending against him. Gumm's confession was so revolting most of it is unprintable. He admitted he was the man who was seen watching the girl from behind a tree the evening prior to the murder. It was a much disputed point whether or not there was any basis for this report, but his confession cleared that point.

This act gave the officers practically their only clue. The Negro had left a hell print near the tree, and this print was dug up and kept in a refrigerator. Yesterday a plaster cast of the heel of one of the shoes worn by Gumm was made, and when confronted with this impression and the print left near the tree, the Negro realized the hopelessness of trying to hold out any longer.

The stenographer was in the counsel room where the Negro was being examined for two hours and was called back at 7:30 p.m., remaining for another hour. At 8:45 p.m., the officers sent out for food and at 9:45 p.m., the group of inquisitors gradually broke up, so as not to give a hint the Negro had confessed. The Negro was taken out of the room, chained to F.C. Dobbs of St. Joe, Superintendent of the police department's bureau of identification.

Dobb had played an important role in the case. S.T. Spade and M. Archer were at the party with Police Chauffeur, P.T. Thong. Gumm was taken down the jury's stairway at the courthouse. Possibly not a resident other than the officers knew. News of the confession was not made public until it was known the St. Joe authorities had the prison far enough away that there could be no longer a threat of mob violence.

A newspaper correspondent was the only person other than the authorities who were aware the prisoner had confessed. He followed the police car the entire distance back to St. Joe, stopping along the roadside to telephone the news to the city. The Negro denied he went to the schoolhouse on the day of the crime with the intention of harming the teacher. He admitted having watched her the evening prior to the slaying. He had a history of hunting and trapping in the vicinity to a great degree.

On the day of the killing, he approached the schoolyard from a field to the north and came around the rear of the schoolhouse. He rounded the corner of the building to pass by the door. Just as he passed in front of the door, the young teacher started for a bucket of coal. She confronted the grinning Negro as she opened the door. Her horror was probably multiplied by having received a glimpse of the same man as he watched her from his vantage point the previous evening. She screamed.

The scream caused her death if the Negro is to be believed. The scream turned a harmless person into a torturer. It instilled the resolve to do her bodily harm. He realized the girl couldn't get away, like a cat with a mouse. When school directors installed wire gratings over the windows a year before, they had unwittingly shut off any escape. The frightened girl ran to the front of the room, her assailant following. She grabbed a broom, the only weapon she could find in the schoolroom.

When the Negro tried to grab it, she bit him on the thumb. The Negro was angered with his bitten thumb, and the girl was not to die without fiendish torture. He dragged her under the edge of a seat and into the aisle. Then he stood watching her. She attempted to raise herself to her feet. "Water," she begged, "won't you please give me a glass of water?"

The killer's club again descended on the brown-thatched head of the teacher and she fell. This blow caused a severe fracture of the skull, partially exposing her brain through an opening. Still, it is doubtful if death was instantaneous with this blow. Then the fiendish nature of the crime became more apparent. Not content with mere murder, the killer abused and mutilated the girl's body, stripping off most of her clothing.

The killer must have been in the building for more than an hour and it is probable several persons passed by the schoolhouse at the time the madman was performing his butcheries. The investigation of Gumm showed the door of the schoolhouse was closed a 4:15 p.m. and 4:30 p.m., but it was open at 5 p.m. It was closed when H.T. Sampson arrived at the building with a lantern at 6 p.m., searching for the girl. She never before had failed to return from school by that time.

The Negro was horrified by the amount of blood on the floor of the school. He took the girl's coat, attempting to mop the floor with it, but he realized this would be futile. His first thought was to dispose of the girl's body. He planned to remove it from the building under cover of darkness. Then he changed his plan. He peered through the half-opened door, saw no one near, and fled.

The authorities could find no one who recalled seeing Gumm the day following the murder, which was suspicious. But yesterday, a city officer saw him and brought him before the authorities. Gumm washed his bloody gloves on his way back after the murder, stopping along a little creed and breaking the ice. He went directly to his home, arriving there about the time the murder was discovered.

He seemed to be a little agitated but not by reason of his atrocious deed, as he attended a school basketball game at 8 p.m. that night. The bloodstained underwear found yesterday near Conception, and which at first was believed to have been worn by the killer, has not been entirely explained, although the apparel did not appear to belong to Gumm.

Since the clothing had been cut with a knife or a pair of scissors, it is now believed possible the garment had been cut up for rages and used in protecting automobile upholstery from blood from rabbits some hunter had thrown in his car. It was learned the area in which the garment was found is a favorite spot with hunters.

Three St. Joe detectives had worked on the case for two full days. They were sent to the scene of the murder the evening of its discovery and remained on the case ever since. Sheriff Harry English, J.P. Johns, prosecuting attorney, and Dr. J.B. Watson, Coroner, were the officials who worked untiringly with the arrest made by L.E. Etherton, a city officer.

Although Gumm was not seen the day following the murder, he had made no effort to leave town and was located yesterday morning after pickup orders had been sent to the principal surrounding cities. The slayer wore gloves during his act of butchering, which accounted for the absence of fingerprints. The details of his confession coincide. He declared that after striking the first blow he dragged his victim out from under the desk where she had fallen. A bloody streak on the floor showed this to be the truth.

Authorities today asked officers in other cities to release all suspects in the case. Suspects had been held at Mount Ayr, Sedalia, Shenandoah, Bedford, and several other places. Every stranger was under suspicion. There were dozens of reports of strange actions of persons unknown to various communities. Detective said from the start they did not believe the killer had escaped any great distance. It was certain he did not have an automobile.

No classes have been held at the Carrott School since the murder of the Teacher, Miss Thelma Holster, Tuesday evening. The school will not be resumed during the next term since there are so few children in the district. The matter of discontinuing the school altogether has been endorsed. In this event, the children would be taken to other schools where the district would pay tuition. There were only five pupils regularly attending the school.

MURDER WEAPON FOUND

Berryville, M.O. Dec. 19-The club with which Reggie Gumm, Negro, beat Miss Thelma Holster, 19-year-old schoolteacher to death Tuesday afternoon, has been found. Returning to a draw in which the Negro told officers last night, he threw the elm stick, 4 ft. long and 1-1/2 inches in diameter. The stick was covered with blood.

It is apparent the route the Negro took on his way home after the murder was such that he retained a view of the school for more than a mile. He did not use a road until he had reached the edge of town. He would have been aware of the murder had been discovered within a few minutes after he left the building.

This morning, officers were searching for the schoolteacher's watch, which the killer said he had thrown away shortly before discarding the club. Officers were satisfied with the finding of the club, which eliminated any chance of Gumm repudiating his confession. He told the authorities last night where the instrument used could be found. Officers had no trouble locating it. With light snow on the ground, it was considered possible the watch would not be found until a thaw. It might be located this afternoon.

A line of men moved forward at once, carefully looking over each foot of the ground. The officers had concealed their purpose to keep away curious onlookers. The club was found a half mile from any road, northeast of the school. The murderer might have escaped in any direction except the northeast because there was no timber or brush to hide in. He would have been visible for some distance along the road which led north of the school.

Apparently, the bloodhounds had never been on his trail. Em Gumm, Reggie's father, refused to believe the charge. "They've got the wrong man!" he said this morning.

Another son spoke, "That wasn't girl's blood on his coat. That was rabbit blood. We all had rabbit blood on our coats just like he did."

The mother was away from home this morning. The family did not seem to realize the seriousness of the charge. Reggie has been in trouble once, sentenced to the penitentiary in 1925 for attempted assault on a girl. Gumm was released after serving his term.

BERRYVILLE NEGOR BROUGHT HERE

St. Joe, M.O. Reggie Gumm, Negro who confessed to killing Miss Thelma Holster, a schoolteacher, is being imprisoned at Central Police Station for fear of mob violence for the second time. The man was brought here on Oct. 21, 1925, after his arrest on a charge of attempted assault on a girl student at the State Teachers College.

Feelings were running high and the sheriff thought it best to put the man under safer guard. Gumm, dressed in khaki trousers, blue shirt, and cap, has on a pair of rubber overshoes, but no shoes, his own having been retained by authorities as evidence. A heel print found at a point where a man was seen watching the schoolteacher prior to the murder matched exactly with a plaster cast of the heel of Gumm's shoes.

Several extra patrolmen were kept in the police station today, in case, an attempt would be made to reach Gumm. He spends his time staring at the walls and ceiling from his cot. He said that he dozed off sometimes. Officers are also on suicide watch. Gumm complained this morning his thumb hurt where he had been bitten by the victim. The thumb was not treated. The Chief of Police did not enter the cage when he was photographed this morning. "I might forget I am an officer of the law," was the only reason given.

CORONER'S JURY VERDICT

"We the undersigned jurors impaneled and sworn on the 16th day of Dec. 1930, at the township of Polk, County of Nowadays, by Dr. J.B. Watson, Coroner, to diligently inquire and true presentment make how and by when Miss Thelma Holster, whose body was found in the Carrott School at 6:30 p.m., on the 16th day of Dec. 1930 came to her death.

"Having viewed and identified the body and heard the evidence, do find the deceased came to her heath from gross injuries to the brain, inflicted with a wooden club by Reginald Gumm, and said Reginald Gumm was the principal before the fact in the perpetration of said felony. Given under our hands this 19th day of Dec. 1930."

GUMM CONFESSES TO MURDER OF TEACHER

Berryville, M.O. De. 19, 1930. Reginald Gumm, 26-year-old Negro ex-convict, confessed last night he had committed the atrocious murder of Miss Thelma Holster in the Carrott School, Tuesday afternoon. With his confession, the terror which has hung like a cloud over this area was lifted. Few people knew yesterday the web of evidence against Gumm was being drawn tighter with each succeeding hour.

Officers rushed him out of town unnoticed when he broke down under the questioning last night. A frozen heel print, coupled with definite knowledge the Negro had been in the vicinity of the school the evening before the crime and he had been convicted of attempted assault on a college girl here in 1924, played prominent roles in the ultimate solution of the crime.

With these clues, officers began searching for Gumm. They were unable to find him until yesterday morning when L.E. Etherton arrested Gumm and two Negro companions as they were hunting in a field northeast of Gumm's home, which is on East Fourth St. The confession was obtained after the Negro had been questioned several hours. It was made by J.P. Johns, prosecuting attorney, and St. Joe detectives. Mr. Johns was in charge.

He drew the revolting story from the man's lips quietly and without the use of violence. Gumm apparently never lost his composure. When he saw the net was tight around him, he told the story willingly, convinced further attempts to deceive his quiet questioner were hopeless. The Negro related how he had walked to the school through the fields. He walked down the fence east of the school, crossed the road into a field south of the school, and then skirted through the fields until he approached the building from the rear. He picked up a heavy club about three feet long on his way.

Miss Holster was correcting papers as Gumm approached. He waited a few moments and then confronted the girl as she opened the door, carrying the coal scuttle.

The girl screamed at the sight of him. He seized her and jerked her into the room. Her watch fell off at the time. She broke away from the intruder, starting to run toward her desk, but the Negro grabbed her again, despite her efforts to beat off the attack with a broom.

Biting her assailant on the thumb, Miss Holster managed to grasp the coal bucket to defend herself. Gumm struck the girl with a stick several times. She fell, pushing one of the desks out of line, and slumped to the floor. He thought the girl was dead, and he dragged her into the aisle. But the girl's life had not yet ended. She warned the Negro her father would soon be there. She asked her attacker for a drink of water and he struck her again with the club.

Frightened of his actions, he then left the school but returned a moment later to deal the final and fatal blow and to finish the crime. He confessed how he watched through a window for his chance to escape. He fled through the schoolyard and returned to town in the same way he had gone out. He had no intention of killing the girl when he went to the school but said when she screamed, he was stimulated to commit the brutal act.

Gumm's confession was not entirely complete, but officers planned to obtain the remainder of it today. His admissions and other evidence to prove his guilt beyond any possible doubt. When arrested, his clothes were stained with blood which he contended was caused by rabbit blood. A plaster cast of his shoe was compared to the heel print found near the school in the frozen earth and matched precisely.

He related to the authorities the exact route he had followed, where he had thrown the stick away, and other details of the crime which were substantiated by subsequent investigation. Mr. Etherton was being praised today for his single-handed capture of the murderer and his two Negro companions, all of whom were armed with shotguns. Etherton saw the Negroes in a field north of Purington station yesterday morning.

Circling around the field, he saw Gumm among the hunters. They changed their direction but Mr. Etherton stopped to talk with them. Just then a rabbit jumped out of a fence-row and Mr. Etherton said, “Fire at him, Reggie!”

Reggie did, and then Mr. Etherton took the men to town having them unload their guns. Gumm’s companions were ‘Shike’ Smith and Ted Gumm, a brother. Mr. Etherton has been assisting the county officers on the case, “What little I could,” he said.

Since the basketball season started at the college, he was employed to assist therein directing traffic at the gymnasium. In this capacity, he was given a badge as a special city officer. Mr. Johns told something of the methods used in solving the crime. He appeared before the coroner’s jury in the courthouse this morning. Expressions of deep gratitude for the prompt solution to the crime were heard on all sides this morning.

CALM RETURNS TO COUNTY

Berryville, M.O. Dec. 20. The excitement has passed. The flames which rose in the hearts of men and women upon learning of the dastardly deed at the Carrott School, Tuesday afternoon, have quieted down, and now the confessed murderer is behind bars, forty miles from the scene of the investigation. Spirited away in the cloak of night in a speeding automobile from any possible chance of mob violence, Reginald Gumm, Negro slayer, and attacker of a white girl, knows only too well what his fate will be.

To those who directed the investigation of the slaying and whose careful handling of the case prevented an outbreak of mob violence, all credit is due. The officers have gone virtually without sleep since the crime was committed. The prosecuting attorney, sheriff, three St. Joe officers, as well as a number of others have worked ceaselessly on a case, which, conceivably, might have taken days or even weeks to solve.

To Dr. Watson, Coroner, and Dr. S.S. Gardner, who gave the officer's valuable assistance in the pathological aspects of the investigation, the authorities are grateful. Leo Etherton and the police are also entitled to credit. All these men left no stone unturned to solve this murder, and their efforts never lagged until the Negro was safely headed to a jail in a nearby county.

It is undeniable there were verbal threats of lynching if the fiend was found, and careful handling of a tense situation can be attributed to the lack of a demonstration. It is, well, the brutal murderer is out of the county. It is certain his doom will be swift. There is no place in society for fiends of such depraved ferocity. The county is breathing easier now. It will breathe still easier when this murderer is definitely removed forever by the law.

Because of his conviction on a charge of attempted assault here in 1925, Reginald Gumm confessed the murderer of Thelma Holster, was suspected immediately after the crime was committed Tuesday evening. The Negro was sentenced to four years in the state penitentiary in

November 1925 for the attempted assault on a Mound City girl who was attending college here. He was released on parole before his term expired and returned to Berryville.

January 21, 1929, in the circuit court of Nowadays County, he was fined $150 for displaying a deadly weapon. Gumm was paroled on bond and on July 30, 1929, was arrested as a suspected prowler but released. The Negro was on parole on the deadly weapon charge until October 6, 1930, when he was discharged from parole.

While here this year, he has worked occasionally on the farm of A.R. Mules. Gumm's police chart from Omaha shows he is 5 ft.-7 ½ inches tall, weighing 123 lbs. Subsequent to his release from prison on the assault charge, he was married but his wife has since died. He lived with his parents on E. 4th St. The theory has suggested Gumm chose a schoolteacher for his victim because of hatred toward teachers growing out of his conviction on the attempted assault charge on a college student in 1925.

Questioned on this point, one city officer said he had a slight recollection of an expression of some such hatred by Gumm. But Lowel Canfield, who was sheriff at the time, said he could not remember Gumm having said, "He would get a schoolteacher yet."

GRUESOME CRIME SOLVED

Berryville, M.O. Dec. 20-The gruesome details of how the body of Thelma Holster, a 20-year-old schoolteacher was found, and the description of the wounds she suffered, was unfolded in the circuit courtroom here this morning when the coroner's jury brought in a verdict that the girl came to her death at the hands of Reginald Gumm, 26-year-old Negro.

Only three witnesses were questioned, Thomas H. Sampson, at whose home Miss Holster lived while teaching school, Dr. J.B. Watson, Coroner, and F.C. Dobbs, St. Joe Detective. The residents of the Carrott School community had grown to love their little schoolteacher in the short time she had taught there. The faltering, low-toned testimony of Mr. Sampson before the coroner's jury attested to this.

His family was worried because Miss Holster stayed after school hours to clean up the one-room school, and he and Mrs. Sampson said Thelma was not afraid and did not change her habit of sweeping the floor and fixing the fire before she left the building.

Tuesday evening when she didn't come home from school, Mr. Sampson said he was worried about Thelma, but Mrs. Sampson was of the opinion the girl was getting ready for the Christmas season and probably would be a little late that night. She was getting the school ready for the Christmas season as shown by the decorations that were on the blackboard, a holly wreathe inside of which 'Merry Christmas' was written. Thelma also was preparing for a joyous Christmas season herself, making presents for the pupils of the school for her relatives and friends, and before her death had sent out Christmas greetings.

When she did not appear at his house, Mr. Sampson said he got a lantern, called his dog, and walked the half-mile north to the school. Whether or not the door was latched, he couldn't say, but it was closed, according to Mr. Sampson's testimony. As he opened the door of the school, it shut off his view of the teacher, but he saw the girl's clothes on the floor and knew that something was wrong.

He entered the building, the light from his lantern showing the teacher lying on the floor, and he was sure no life was left in the body. Going home, Mr. Sampson said he hailed several people along the way, telling them, "Our schoolteacher has been murdered."

Paul Wing, his son-in-law, was taken informed and Mr. Wing and Sheriff English soon arrived at the school, Mr. Sampson said. Dr. Watson was sworn in by Constable Robert Tyree and gave his testimony of how he found the body of Miss Holster in the school with numerous blood spots on the floor, desks, and door, the abrasions on the girl's face, the crushed skull, how the ear was slashed and of the other gashes he found on her body.

The description revealed vividly the fiendishness of the crime committed by the confessed slayer. F.C. Dobbs, St Joe Detective, an elderly man who has been on the police force for over twenty years, told the jurors about the confession.

LEGAL PROSECUTION PROCEEDS

Berryville, M.O. Dec. 20, 1930-The first step in the prosecution of the Negro, Reginald Gumm, who confessed to the murder of Miss Thelma Holster has taken place in the court of the justice of the peace of Polk Township. An affidavit charging murder in the first degree was filed in the office of Phares O. Sullivan, justice of the peace, today by Paul R, Johns, Prosecutor. The affidavit indicates it's the knowledge of the prosecutor that Miss Holster came to her death by blows inflicted on the head by the club in the hands of Reginald Gumm.

After due time is allowed, the defendant will be given a preliminary hearing and the defendant may waive or ask for a hearing so the justice may decide whether there is sufficient evidence to show a felon has been committed. If either is the case, the justice files a transcript of the proceedings with the Justice Court in the circuit court of this county. Then the defendant would be brought for a hearing.

A defendant in a criminal action is permitted to have counsel by the court. The circuit court will convene the second Monday in January and in all likelihood, Gumm will be brought before Judge D.D. Rivers sometime in January on charges of first-degree murder. The sum of $55 toward the fund of $500 started as a reward for the apprehension and conviction of the slayer of Miss Holster, was not augmented today, following the news the slayer confessed.

Individuals who started the movement were strong in the opinion a suitable reward should be offered. A $500 check has been forwarded here and this office will be glad to hold the money for the reward until such a time as the sponsors of the movement see fit to have it distributed. The prosecuting attorney has expressed his gratitude to the members of the detective department of the St. Joe Police who have given their time and efforts freely in aiding to solve the crime. For a time it seemed so baffling. He is especially grateful to Leo Etherton.

ANALYZING CLUES, THE PROSECUTOR PLANS PROSECUTION OF GUMM.

Berryville, M.O. Dec. 21, 1930-Officers followed a chart of directions made by Reggie Gumm, murderer of

Theelma Holster, a 20-year-old schoolteacher who was killed Tuesday afternoon. This morning they found the club Gumm had hit Miss Holster with. The club was founded by Cycle Officer R.P. Wright of St. Joe and a newspaper reporter. Several men went to the schoolhouse shortly after 8:00 a.m.

Looking for the club and a wristwatch that Gumm had taken from Miss Holster, the men went through a fence on the east side of the school. Spreading out in a line, they began walking northeast of the school. All were watching the ground closely for the watch Gumm said he lost after running from the school. Walking north through a pasture, the party crossed a deep ravine. They then went east to a cornfield a quarter of a mile east of the school.

From there, they went north across another ravine. Gumm said he dropped the stick he had used near some trees he thought were willows. He made no effort to hide it. After going some three-quarters of a mile northeast of the school to a place where he crossed two fences in his flight, nothing had been found and officers decided to turn back and search over the same ground they had covered.

The point where the hunt started was where Gumm said he first missed the watch after he had thrown the stick away. Wright and the reporter were going west down a gulley which was thickly covered with long, dead grass when the stick was discovered. An agreement had been made before the hunt started that no one was to pick up either the club or the watch if they were found without calling the rest of the men.

This was done and all the men witnessed the stick being picked up. The stick was found a little more than a half mile northeast of the schoolhouse. The spot is approximately 250 yard west of a fence. The stick is about four feet long and is an old piece of hedge wood. One end of the club was larger than the other due to a knot, and this end was covered with blood and had some human hair on it. The entire stick was smeared with blood.

The men in the search started back toward the school, still looking for the watch, but snow on the ground hampered the hunt. The watch was not found. Search for it was resumed in the afternoon.

MOB IN ST. JOE SATURDAY NIGHT LEAVES WITHOUT VIOLENCE. GUARDSMEN CALLED OUT. ST. JOE AUTHORITIES PROVE FULLY PREPARED TO QUELL DISTURBANCE. NO MORE TROUBLE EXPECTED.

Bulletin: Prosecuting Attorney Denied A Report Reginald Gumm Recanted Confession.

Berryville, MO. Dec. 21, 1930-Reports from St. Joe that Reginald Gumm has been taken by authorities to Jeff City from the Buckcannon County jail at St Joe has been received. The chance for any mob violence was greatly diminished today, following the gathering of a mob of 2 or more at St. Joe, Saturday night. The report Gumm had been moved to Jeff City was received from Buckcannon County Sheriff, J.I. Hickock.

One level-headed man in the gathering was credited with playing a big role in the decision to disperse the mob. The man, who was a Nowadays county citizen, urged the others to return home. "The officers of St. Joe," he declared, "have done us a neighborly act. They came to our town and helped us solve this terrible murder. Let's not do anything that might bring disgrace to their town."

This speech seemed to have been immediately effective and the sense of fairness in the group began to make itself felt. Shortly afterward, the members of the mob began to leave and by about 3 a.m. had practically dispersed.

NEGRO MURDERER IS CHAINED TO THE ROOF OF CARROTT SCHOOL AND BURNED ALIVE BY MOB. Reginald Gumm, 27-year-old Negro, Confessed Slayer, Pays Penalty in Flames of School Where Teacher Was Brutally Murdered, Orderly Crowd Watches the Mob's Actions. Negro Taken From Sheriff English at East Door of the Courthouse; Led by Chain to His Doom. The building is saturated with gasoline. Negro Chained to Roof Before Match is Touched to Building.

Berryville, MO. Jan. 12, 1931. Reginald Gumm, Negro, paid the ultimate price for his confessed crime on a Nowadays County schoolteacher. He was burned to death and chained to the top of the school where he committed his confessed crime at 10:30 a.m. as an orderly crowd of nearly 3,000 calmly watched. Gumm confessed another Negro, 'Shike' Smith, was implicated in the killing of Miss Thelma Holster. Gumm was taken away from Sheriff Harry English at about 9:30 a.m. as he was being brought to the courthouse from the jail.

The Negro walked the entire distance to the Carrott School, three miles southwest, led by a chain. It was an orderly mob that took charge of the affair. The thousands who gathered at the school looked on curiously without any attempt being made to interfere. There was no attempt by any person or parties to check the mob once it had Gumm in its possession. The leaders of the mob seemed to be in no hurry. Their plans were well organized.

Gumm did not attempt to get away. It would have been a useless move on the part of the Negro. He was taken into the Carrott School, where the leaders questioned the Negro and seemed to be satisfied with the confession Gumm made. Before the mob had arrived at the school, preparations had been made by others who seemed to be in on the plans.

The equipment of the school building was removed, even to the slates on the wall. An improvised ladder was used to hoist Gumm on top of the building. He was pulled up on the roof by means of a long chain. The leader tore the shingles off of the roof and then poured high-test gasoline around his body and on the roof. In the meantime, gas was poured over the floor of the school and when a match was touched to it, the building went up in flames.

The National Guard was subject to call from the sheriff but the commander here was not notified and was not called out to protect the Negro. It was a motive of revenge to make the black man pay for his terrible, most atrocious deed that he committed upon the simple, pure schoolteacher who met her death at the age of 20 years.

There was a stir around town last night. The biggest crowd in the history of the town on a normal Sunday was said to have been here. The restaurants were filled. Cars bringing people from every direction were here. But they kept coming. This morning, as early as 4 a.m., others began to come. It had been announced Gumm would be brought here to be arraigned at 9 a.m. this morning.

Gumm was brought from the jail at Kansas City, Saturday night. It was said by a deputy this morning, the car bringing Gumm, in which there was Sheriff English and his deputies, arrived here at 8:30 p.m. Saturday night. Watchers were on the lookout all night around the courthouse and jail, and it was rumored around the city that the Negro was kept in the Farmers Trust Company over Sunday.

However, deputies said the Negro was kept in jail. It was a huge crowd that gathered in the courtroom as early as 7 a.m. this morning. By the time Judge Rivers arrived, the room was jammed, the corridors packed, and the downstairs corridors were filled. There were whispers current, "Now is the time to get him."

When Judge Rivers called the court, the prosecuting attorney walked forward, whispered to the judge, and then the sheriff was ordered to bring the Negro into court. The crowd waited in anticipation. It was sensed something was going to happen. All of a sudden the crowd lurched forward to the north windows of the courthouse. The crowd rushed out as fast as possible. But the sheriff never got the Negro into the courthouse.

It was said that the officer who was in the car with the Negro hit a man over the head who tried to grab the Negro, but in a jiffy, the policeman was knocked down and carried away. The crowd with the Negro surged toward Third St. They went toward a truck, but instead of taking the Negro to the car, walked him south, then west down first St., out past the country club, and then through a field toward the little school.

NATIONAL GUARD STAYED IN THE ARMORY

St. Louis, M.O. Jan. 12-Adj. Gen A.V. Pershing, Commander of the National Guard, told newspapers by telephone sixty armed and uniformed National Guardsmen were drilling today at the Armory, a block from the courthouse, when Reginald Gumm, Negro, accused of the murder of Miss Thelma Holster, was taken from the sheriff and his deputies by a mob. The Adj. Gen. had been sent by Gov.

Davis to take charge of local guardsmen. "My men could do nothing until the county authorities asked for assistance," Gen. Pershing said. "No request for help has yet been made. We did not even learn a mob had taken the prisoner until sometime later when they were already started for the schoolhouse."

Gen. Pershing had conferred with Sheriff English after his arrival yesterday afternoon and the sheriff had told him he expected trouble. It was arranged for Battery C of the 128th Field Artillery Unit to be held in readiness at the Armory. It could be summoned by messenger or by telephone. The courthouse cannot be seen from the Armory, but those in the Armory shortly after 9 a.m. noticed men running toward the courthouse.

When the commotion had subsided, militiamen walked out and learned what had taken place. Gov. Davis at Jeff City said he would not be able to discuss anything until he received full reports of what occurred. "This is a horrible thing, but I don't want to commit or outline a course of action until I know all the facts," he said.

Before Gen. Pershing made his statement, Sheriff English had declared over the telephone he was unaware of a mobilized unit of the National Guard at the armory. When reporters sought to question English, his wife answered the telephone and said the sheriff did not want to make any further statement. English declined to say whether he recognized any of the mob. If their identities are learned, they will be prosecuted, said the prosecuting attorney. Reporters talked to Gen.

Pershing shortly before 9 a.m. this morning. He had been authorized to call the guard only if the sheriff asked for assistance. About fifty militiamen were lined up in the Armory. Reporters left the building shortly afterward, and within a few minutes, the mob had taken Gumm away from the sheriff.

NEGRO BURNED BY MOB ON SCHOOLHOUSE ROOF.

Teacher Found Dead in School on December 16. Her body was discovered by T.H. Sampson at the Carrott School. She Had Been Clubbed and the Body Was Torn.

Berryville, M.O. Jan. 12-Miss Thelma Holster, daughter of Mr. and Mrs. George Holster, was found dead in the Carrott School building, of which she was the teacher, about 6:30 p.m. the night of December 16, 1930. Her body was found by T.H. Sampson, a farmer, who lives south of the school and with whom she boarded.

The search was made for the girl when she did not return for the evening meal. Bloodhounds were brought to the Carrott School that night and again the next morning. The dogs took up trails to two nearby farms housed, but the investigation would not substantiate the theory that the probable killer had been or lived at either.

Detectives of the Bertillon staff of the St. Joe Police Department were assigned to the case and gave all their time until the slayer confessed. They assisted Nowadays County authorities in solving the case, even when there were no definite clues that could be followed up in tracking the slayer of the 2-year-old schoolteacher.

However, officers had noticed a certain Negro, who had served time in the Missouri Prison for an attempted assault on a college girl from Mound City, had been back lately. Working on suspicion, the officers considered Reginald Gumm, who was 27 years old on January 10, 1931, as a suspect. He had not been seen on Wednesday, following the murder, but was picked up by Special Officer Leo Etherton in a cornfield on the northeast edge of the city on Thursday morning.

Gumm, the son of Mr. And Mrs. Em Gumm, was questioned all afternoon and shortly after 6 p.m., made a confession and signed a written statement to the effect he killed Miss Holster. He was rushed immediately to the city jail at St. Joe. The next day, he was transferred to the Buckcannon County jail at St. Joe. After a demonstration around the jail, he was removed from the Jackson County Jail in Kansas City. Once before, Gumm was taken to St Joe to avoid possible mob violence in October 1925, when he was arrested on an attempted assault charge.

In November 1925, Gumm was convicted of the attempted assault charge and was sentenced to four years in state prison. He was discharged under the merit system on

January 28, 1928. Since then, he was charged with carrying a concealed weapon, and his discharge of parole from the circuit court was ordered in the October 1930, term of the court.

In making his confession, the Negro told of the gruesome crime, relating events which made the officers certain his confession was true. On the afternoon of Dec. 15, 1930, Gumm declared he was looking for a place to start a trapline in the area of the Carrott School, substantiating the report of a nearby farmer, William Oldy, who said he saw a stranger stalking in the vicinity after the school was dismissed. Gumm told of going out in the same area the next day, picking up a hedge wood club, and entering the school after the children had gone home. He clubbed the teacher over the head and beat her to death when she fought him back and bit his thumb.

Although Gumm declared he did not attack the girl, the inquest by the coroner revealed the girl was attacked and cut up after she had been murdered. Gumm lived in Omaha after being released from prison. However, before going to Omaha, he married a Negro girl, who died while in Omaha.

In Omaha, he was arrested on July 30, 1929, as a suspected prowler, but was released. Since his arrest on the first-degree murder charge, attempts have been made to connect Gumm with the Omaha ax murders, but nothing definite has been confirmed.

The Negro's victim was a former student at the State Teachers College here, and was buried at Clermont, Nowadays County, the day Gumm made his confession. She had a 60 hr teacher's certificate, comparable to two years' work at the institution. She was born near Clermont and had lived with her parents when they lived in Berryville. This was her first year of teaching school. She is survived by her parents, a brother Orville, of Barnyard, and a sister, Mrs. Enis Payne, Pickers, M.O. Mr. Johns who was in charge of the investigation would not be assisting in the prosecution as his term expired Dec. 31, 1930.

Virgil Stern, elected in Nov. 1930, took office the first of the year. He would have been assisted in the trial of Gumm, if he had demanded a trial, by P. Mason, attorney, who is associated with former State Senator M.E. Sharp. Mr. Mason was a prosecutor when Gumm was sentenced in 1925 to state prison. He was prosecuting attorney for four terms.

His first case in 1911 was that of Hez Rosco, who was convicted and hanged for the killing of the Ova Hubbell family. It was said this morning in regard to the mob action that "for the sake of law, order, and good citizenship, it was a most regrettable incident." Sheriff Harry English was home in bed when reached by a reporter. He said his right arm was severely damaged when the leaders of the mob jerked the handcuffs away from him. He said his shoulders and back were also severely sprained.

The statement made by Sheriff English was that he was "very sorry it all happened and hated it very much." He said the three other officers in the car with him did their best to protect Gumm, but the mob was too strong and they could not be held back. Reginald Gumm, the Negro who paid with his life for his confessed murder of Miss Thelma Holster, schoolteacher, was apparently unterrified when he went to his doom in the flames this morning.

Even until the last, when he was being chained down to the roof of the Carrott School, where Thelma Holster was murdered, he did not shrink, did not fight, but followed all the directions of those who had him in charge. Gumm has not pulled up the ladder to his doom. Instead, he climbed up the steps of the improvised ladder. The top rung broke under his weight.

The Negro caught himself and pulled himself to the top. It was remarked that not many would have walked the entire distance in his condition. It was surprising the Negro was not dead by the time the mob reached the school, thinking the mob would have to drag him; but not Gumm.

He walked steadily along at the end of the chain without any resistance, or without being beaten. There were many clubs in evidence but he went without being dragged or prodded. Down 1st St., the leaders of the mob took Gumm. Those close to the leaders said when they crossed Mulberry St., Gumm told of another Negro being involved.

Early in the death march, the Negro begged for his life, but soon saw this was hopeless. On went the mob, which was bent on its rightful mission. It was organized efficiently. There were persons who formed a square around the Negro. Watchers with clubs were on the outskirts of the crowd. Any person who advanced in front of the crowd was checked. No automobile was allowed to proceed ahead of the crowd after it had arrived at the field where it cut across to the schoolhouse.

Further evidence the plans were well laid was shown when men went in advance to clear out the schoolhouse so the building would not be slowly burning. Hundreds, hearing the 'mob had got the Negro', rushed to their cars and drove out to the schoolhouse. It was definitely known they would go to the schoolhouse. When questions were asked at the school: “Where’s the Negro? Are you sure they are going to bring him here?” somebody else would say, “We passed the crowd as we came out”.

Slowly but surely, the mob advanced. Hundreds of curious trailed along to see what would happen. Who were these people? Nobody knew these strangers. There were many strangers in town this morning. People never before seen in working clothing, high-top boots, overalls, and leather coats ran in the corridors of the courthouse. They stayed on the first floor for the most part. People whispered, “I’ll watch here.”

Last night there were so many people in town, they had to stand all night on the streets. In the morning, they were still here. They felt like something had to happen and they weren’t disappointed. Rumors became widespread today that Gumm said, just before he was lynched, ‘Shike’ Smith was with him at the time of the murder of Miss Holster, and that ‘Shike’ struck one of the blows that killed the girl. B.B. Skinner, Assessor of Polk Township said this afternoon, he saw Smith the afternoon of the murder.

Mr. Skinner said he went to the home of Frank Snodgrass on west 5th St. Shortly before 5 p.m. On Tuesday, Dec. 16. While in the basement, he talked to Smith, who was working around the house. Gumm, in his confession, said he (Gumm) was in the schoolhouse at the time the Dudlow girl rode past the building. The time was fixed at 5 p.m. or a little later when Smith was at the Snodgrass home.

LYNCHINGS IN MISSOURI ON THE RISE

Berryville, M.O. Jan. 16, 1931-The lynching of Reginald Gumm was the sixth in Missouri in the last ten years. In each case, the victim was a Negro accused of assault or attempted assault, and there was no legal prosecution.

At Bowling Blue in 1921, Roy Hammer was hanged from a bridge for an attempted attack on a 15-year-old white girl. At Charlestown in 1924, Roosevelt Gigger was hanged and burned for attempted assault on a 15-year-old white girl. In Extra Springs in 1925, Walter Michaels was hanged after a shot on an improvised scaffold for attacking a white woman.

The mob was evidently led by people who had carefully mapped out their plans. Gumm was shackled with a chain about ten feet long. He said nothing to his captors. Some of them shouted, "To hell with the law," as they approached the school building. About 500 men were in the group immediately around the prisoner. Some cars had gone to the school immediately after the mob seized Gumm.

More than a thousand people, including some women and children, were on the scene of the lynching long before the mob appeared. Many milled around in the cold and many suggested the lynching was to take place somewhere else. When at last the mob appeared, crossing the fields northeast of the school, many of the spectators ran across the fields to meet them.

The leaders evidently decided to walk to the school in order that they could forestall any possible move to recapture the Negro. Many in the mob carried clubs. As they neared the school, a number of them pushed cars parked in the field out of the path of the mob. Automobiles continued to rush to the scene even after the blaze was started. Cars were parked on both sides of the road. The spectators began to shout as the lynching party approached and many of them yelled insistently that the Negro be placed on the roof where all could see.

When Gumm was taken inside the building, some men who took the Negro inside assured the crowd they would bring Gumm out as soon as they heard a confession. Several men were on the roof. They tore some shingles off in order to run the Negro's chains around the rafters. Others began to break the windowpanes out while one man sprinkled gasoline around the inside of the building. An improvised ladder had been placed there. Three leaders of the mob went up the ladder before Gumm. They carried the chain and Gumm followed.

Holes were made in the roof on both sides of the ridge pole and the chains were run through these. Gumm evidently made no sound as he was chained down and gasoline was sprinkled all around him. A thick cloud of black smoke arose within a second or two of the time the match was lighted. This converted the Carrott School into a funeral pyre.

The crowd became almost silent as the flames began to rise. The thick smoke was fueled by the cold north wind. Occasional glimpses of the writhing form of the Negro could be seen. The match was applied at about 10:35 a.m. His body showed blistering skin, splotched white patches of exposed flesh, and hair burning like a torch.

By 10:44 a.m., it was evident the Negro was dead. His writing ceased as he slumped. His muscles tensed in the rigidity of death across the ridgepole. His flesh was seared white before the end came. It gave the appearance of a mummy. The crowd began to leave as the flames rose. It was evident their desire for vengeance for the brutal murder of the schoolteacher had been realized.

The school's roof collapsed and was completely destroyed. The body of the Negro fell into the ashes of the schoolhouse. Remnants of the school were taken away by members of the crowd as souvenirs. The black race was represented today by one person only. His ashes now remain at the Carrott School. The Negro folks, sensing a disturbance, kept themselves out of sight. Only one family stayed here since the murder of Thelma Holster. Not a colored person was to be seen on the streets today. It is understood that twenty-two of the race left since Reginald Gumm confessed he committed murder.

MISSOURI LEGISLATURE ADOPTS COMDENATION RESOLUTION

Jeff City, M.O. Jan. 21, 1931-The House of the legislature today adopted a resolution condemning the lynching of Reginald Gumm, Negro, Monday and urged any local official derelict in duty in connection with the affair to be punished. The resolution introduced by Rep. I.P. Freely, Tanney County, followed the action of the House, Tuesday, in postponing a resolution for a search investigation by state officials of the lynching.

The resolution adopted today without debate: "Whereas the indefinite postponement of the resolution condemning the recent mob action has been misconstrued by some as an apology for the action of the mob. Therefore, be it resolved by the House of Representatives, that we hereby condemn the barbarous action of the mob and urge all officers charged with responsibility for law and order to use their utmost endeavor to bring the offenders to justice and especially to punish any officer if found derelict in his duty in defending and protecting the prisoner in his charge."

The Attorney General today ordered a special investigator from his office to inquire into the lynching of Reginald Gumm, Negro, by a mob Monday morning. The Attorney General ordered the inquiry upon request of the governor who spent the morning in conference with Adj. Gen. J.J. Pershing, who was in command of National Guard troops assembled to prevent the lynching.

Gen. Pershing was holding one company of troops in the armory awaiting a call from Sheriff Harry English of Nowadays County. The troops never were called, Gen. Pershing reported to the chief executive. The governor would not reveal the identity of the special investigator. The inquiry will be started at once, he said.

The investigation report will be made direct to the governor and attorney general, who then will determine what further action will be taken. The investigator will inquire particularly into the leadership of the mob and the action of county officials. It was said, "The governor will announce Gen. Pershing's report when it has been prepared."

Jan. 15, 1931-Mob Lynches Negro, State Militia But Block Away, Sheriff Says He Failed to Act for Fear Someone Would Be Killed; Funeral Pyre of Reginald Gumm Who Died at Hands of Mob.

Washington, D.C., Jan. 15, 1931. MOB BURNS KILLER OF SCHOOLTEACHER.

Chicago, IL., Jan. 15, 1931. MOB CREMATES MAN. TROOPS DRILL BLOCK AWAY AS CANNIBALS DISGRACE STATE. THE TORCH OF CIVILIZATION IN MISSOURI.

Summary of Periodical Accounts

At the time of Thelma's death, photographs of the Carrott Schoolhouse were published in local and regional newspapers, both from the outside and inside, depicting the arrangement of buildings, trees, and the spot where Thelma was found, absent her body. At the time of Reggie's death, no photos were allowed by the organizers of the lynching to be taken, but several appeared in print over the next few days in several newspapers.

It should be noted that one crew of reporters from Omaha took several photos of the Carrott Schoolhouse just a few hours before the mob arrived with Reggie. There were no trees or outbuildings or massive crowds visible, while a scaffold ladder was shown to have been built on the side of the schoolhouse. Kansas City newspapers showed some of the crowd arriving with Gumm and the remains of the schoolhouse foundation several hours after the fire was out.

Upon closer inspection of photos purporting to show the schoolhouse on fire, which were supposedly leaked to the press, they appear to have been 'doctored' so as to give the impression the incident did take place as described in the written accounts, only with trees and outbuildings present and absent a scaffold ladder, and which it would be impossible to see anyone on top of the schoolhouse, or to identify any of the people standing around the school.

After Reggie was arrested, the accounts in the papers painted him guilty as charged, but over the next three weeks, most articles seemed to gradually imply restraint from lynching scenarios and reinforced the rationale for the rule of law in the public mind. Obviously, this was never entirely achieved, as long-held myths that all 'black' people were bad, and couldn't be trusted around 'white' women, was coupled with the notion that the slow and slippery wheels of the justice system could be manipulated to let guilty people go free.

Public accounts also tried to portray the authorities as exemplary and above reproach as they were doing all that was humanly possible to capture Thelma's killer.

After Reggie's arrest, the authorities were portrayed as trying to do all that the law required of a civilized society to ensure justice was achieved according to accepted standards of law enforcement practice and jurisprudence. But the 'rush to judgment' mentality had already taken hold of the general populace in a continuation of the mass hysteria mode that had held an invisible 'death grip' on the collective conscious of the people since news of Thelma's death nearly a month before.

Either the ministers of propaganda didn't realize they were riding a whirlwind until it was too late, or they knew all along what was going on from an insider informant in the sheriff's or prosecuting attorney's power structure. They most likely wanted the outcome that would eventually engulf the Carrott Schoolhouse and the community in a bonanza of publicity. I'm inclined to believe most publishers blamed the editors, who in turn blamed the unnamed reporters, who just wanted to get the scoop and keep their jobs, taking the money, or may even have had other ulterior motives. It only takes one Judas.

At first, newspaper accounts were replete with misinformation intended to sell papers by use of vague, false, and misleading rumors passed off as statements of fact and amounted to cheap sensationalism. They inflamed the senses of the public into a blind rage and cast suspicion on anyone who didn't conform to accepted social standards or might have had a hand in Thelma's death.

No one seemed to know which one was which, just wanting to capture the guilty party as soon as possible, before they got away, and bring them to justice whatever that might include. None of the reports had published identified authors. And, I could not find any record of the National Guard or Attorney General investigation reports that were supposed to be released by the governor after they were prepared.

Eyewitnesses

Living eyewitnesses (104) I interviewed, most of them between 1976-1979 while I was in graduate school, only agreed to discuss what they knew about the incident because they knew I was the great-grandson of a well-respected local family who would do nothing to jeopardize their standing in the community, and it would help me with a term paper I was writing in the Psychology of Group Behavior.

For them, about fifty years earlier, it was desperate times for desperate people, trying to take care of themselves and their own; far different from anything I had ever known. Many I tried to interview who were lifelong residents of the county and were alive at the time of the 'burning' incident, chose not to be interviewed, for whatever stated or unstated reason.

On the evening of Dec. 15, 1930, Ruthie M. (age 29 the day before Thelma's murder, age 79 at the time of the interview) was talking to her mother on a party phone line at about 6 p.m. Suddenly, an unknown young woman's voice broke in on the line insisting it was an emergency and wanted to be connected with the sheriff. After hanging up to allow the operator to connect them, Ruthie picked up the phone a few minutes later, secretly listening in on the conversation.

The young woman was calling to report a suspicious character following her home after school. She said she didn't recognize the person several yards behind her, as it was just after sundown, but described someone of medium height and build, wearing a hunting coat and cap. She thought it was a man but didn't indicate whether he was black or white, fat or thin, unspoken, or whether armed or not. Her voice was so high-pitched and rapid, it was difficult to understand all she was saying.

Ruthie thought the woman was going into hysterics when the sheriff reassured her he would look into the matter and hung up. Ruthie called her mother back later and asked who was on the phone.

"That was our new teacher, Thelma Holster!" her mother insisted. Ruthie became frightened so much so that she went to the sheriff's office the following morning to see if anything had been done. She said the sheriff felt it was a case of an over-anxious young woman being unexpectedly surprised by a hunter setting a trap line; nothing to worry about.

On all accounts of Thelma's crime scene, August S. in 1977 was the most detailed (he had two older sisters, June and July). He was 14 in December 1930 (61 at the time of our interview), lucid in conversation, and sharp as a tack. He stated that on Dec. 16, 1930; he was driving a team of mules and wagon home from the fields just after sundown when a local farmer carrying a lantern ran out of the Carrott Schoolhouse toward the road, yelling at August to stop and wait at the school while the farmer called the sheriff. "Someone killed our little teacher! Don't let anyone in the school!" the farmer said.

Using the lantern while waiting for the farmer to return with the sheriff, he looked inside one of the windows that weren't completely covered with Christmas decorations. There, in the middle of the floor near the front door in a pool of blood, was the nude body of Thelma Holster. "Laying on her stomach, sort of, with her head turned toward me, her eyes still open but not moving," he said.

Right-to-right, left-to-left, her wrists had been tied to her ankles. "She was hog-tied with her behind sticking up," he exclaimed. "She looked like a frog trying to jump only to land on her face."

She was covered in blood with several cuts noted all over her body and gagged with a strip of cloth suggesting to him she had been beaten, raped, stabbed, and killed in the 'Negroid Way'. After about 15 minutes of waiting and before anyone else came back to the schoolhouse, his sister June came looking for him and told him, "Pa says come home right now!" which he did without hesitation, setting the lantern down at the schoolhouse front door.

At the time, I had never heard or read of any such dastardly scene described in such a 'child-like' manner, nor had I found any professional authority who could explain his 'Negroid Way' phrasing.

Since that time, I have found references to religious rituals in third-world subcultures that were similar to his description while participants were possibly under some sort of drug-induced trance and chanting allegiance to a deity. He denied having gone inside the school, as the front door was closed, but about a half hour later while looking out the attic window from his home, he saw several people arrive at the schoolhouse, including the farmer and eventually the sheriff and county coroner who started investigating. Searching for two days, few clues of any major significance were publicly announced as found by authorities.

The best and most complete eyewitness account of the events after Thelma's death was recounted to me by granddad's second cousin, Mabel C. (age 70 at the time of the interview and 20 years old at the time of the burning; us kids called her 'Aunt Mabel'). She stated the sheriff was good old Uncle Harry, age 63 at the time of the episode that would change everyone's life, and married to Mabel's grandmother's sister.

"On Dec. 18, 1930, an auxiliary city policeman brought Reggie and two other hunters in for questioning," she said. Remembering they had been questioned and released the evening of Thelma's murder, they had admitted they had been in the area on the day in question. Reggie had a prior criminal record of arrests for minor offenses and one conviction for attempted assault on a white co-ed teacher-in-training at a local state teachers' college in September 1925.

"After confronting him with what evidence they had and several hours of interrogation, Reggie admitted to the crime and signed a confession," she said.

The other hunters, as well as several other suspicious characters, were released. News of an arrest in the case spread like 'ants uncovered from a big rock', just as the original news of a teacher being murdered had. Even those held in the highest esteem were reflexively catapulted thru shock, bewilderment, fear, and panic on an emotional roller coaster ride for two days after the news of Thelma's killing.

Calls for the apprehension of the criminal(s) responsible and vengeance grew bolder with each passing hour. The ride would seem to be over when an equally exacting act of retribution achieved a life sentence for her killer. In actuality, it wouldn't be over for some time after the county declared war on one Reginald Gumm for the alleged murder of Thelma Holster.

"Uncle Harry transported Reggie forty miles south to Buckhannon County," she said, much to the dismay of the general populace. "When the law failed to protect all the citizens of our fair land, they felt doing it themselves was the only way. After all, they held their principles above any personal gain."

She related that on the evening of Saturday, Dec. 20, 1930, two days after Reggie was arrested and moved to St. Joe, a mob of about 200 civilians, torches and weapons of all kinds in hand, surrounded the St. Joe City Jail. A truck with a mounted machine gun had been backed up to the front door of the jail by authorities. The 'white' vigilantes started to enter when a member of the crowd stepped forward and parted the crowd like 'Moses at the Red Sea'.

He reasoned with the mob to disperse, admonishing them to let the law take its course and not to cast shame on a neighboring county that had done all it could to bring the killer of Thelma to justice in the first place. "Vengeance for Thelma will be achieved in Nowadays County, the same way it was for others who killed the innocent without mercy; on the gallows," he said.

"It was Mickey! He was a Mason, too, don't you know," she said.

On a bone cold snowy January 12, 1931, nearly a month after Thelma died, a mob would try a second time to avenge her murder. News Reggie had been brought back to Berryville at about 3:30 a.m., on December 26, 1930, for an arraignment without public knowledge, inflamed the passions of the county even worse. He waved his right to a preliminary trial and a formal trial date was set for January 12, 1931.

Newspapers reported that Reggie had been transferred to the state Penitentiary in Jeff City, to prevent any chance of mob violence. In fact, he had been transferred to the

Jackson County Jail in Kansas City. When members of the community found out the truth, they felt betrayed and the temptation would be too great on January 12, 1931. Justice would not be denied by a bunch of smooth, fast-talking lawyers from the city, as they felt it had been in 1925.

Of all the actual witnesses I spoke with, Marie B., (age 72 at the time of the interview, and age 24 at the time of the 'burning' incident), gave me the most objective and definitive report on the abduction of Reggie. On the morning of Jan. 12, 1931, she was standing in a second-floor window of her husband's law office above Woolworth's.

Overlooking the entire courthouse square at about 9 a.m., she heard a commotion and saw a vast throng of people below her gathered around the courthouse.

"Not a wagon could move anywhere on the square," she said. She estimated the crowd to be about 2,000 strong. Every storefront and second-floor window had someone in it yelling, gesturing with their arms, and brandishing weapons of various kinds with the crowd. Men, women, and children, it was like nothing she had ever seen before, or since.

The sheriff, Reggie, and three deputies slowly drove up to the east door entrance of the courthouse from the county jail, occasionally honking at people to get out of the way. Missouri Governor Davis, fearing mob violence and at the request of several local business and county government leaders, had ordered a unit of the National Guard to be quartered and drilled just a block away at the old armory, what is now the public library, in the event they were needed to enforce compliance with state law.

All at once when the sheriff tried to go in the east courthouse entrance, the crowd closed in on them, grabbing Reggie and beating the sheriff, his deputies, and anyone who tried to resist them. Years later, other witnesses stated the leader of the mob told the sheriff, "Either you move out of the way or die with this man. Either way, he's going to die today."

No one asked for the guard unit to intervene; not a shot was fired. Leaders of the mob would be later rumored to be local citizens but the leader of the group was only identified as 'an outsider in a red coat'. They surrounded Reggie in a small human square, trying unsuccessfully to restrain the crowd.

Clasping his hands with a bull chain and leading him across the southwest corner of the courthouse lawn, she saw him stripped of his clothes, hit and cut with just about every object anyone had, spit on, cursed, and spared no form of cruelty, including castration.

"He had the largest penis I ever saw on a man. He had to grasp the end of what was left between his fingers to keep from bleeding to death while he was led south down Main St. to 1st. St., past the Methodist Church where Thelma's funeral had been held and then west toward the Carrott School, out of my sight," she remarked.

She claimed she didn't know anyone in the crowd but saw many jump in their cars and trucks, trying to rush out to the schoolhouse ahead of the mob. She stated she did not go with the crowd but rather went to check on her husband, who was in the courtroom of the courthouse waiting for the trial to get underway.

“I was told later that after walking over fields and back roads in spotty ankle-deep snow, twelve men briefly held a ‘kangaroo’ court inside the school at which time Reggie confessed to killing Thelma, claiming Paul ‘Shike’ Smith had a hand in the crime, followed by a unanimous vote to cremate him while chained to the ridge pole rafter of the school,” she said.

The building had already been emptied of all usable equipment and supplies, and a scaffold ladder with handrails had been built on the east side of the building with holes in the roof for ventilation. A man in a red coat tossed a lit piece of paper into the school after Reggie had been chained to the roof, and in the process, destroyed Thelma’s crime scene and created another on the same spot.

After finding her husband in the courthouse, they were walking back to his offices when they saw the mob returning. The mob marched directly east down 4h St. to the Gumm residence.

“They burned down the Gumm home, too,” she said, which had been abandoned along with several other shacks in the neighborhood shortly after Reggie had signed his confession back in Dec. “I’ve got a piece of the schoolhouse if you’d like to see it,” she said.

I thanked her for her input without questioning her about how she came to have it and returned home to a restless night’s sleep.

Hazel F., age 18 at the time of the incident and one of grandma’s closest friends stated that on the evening of January 14, 1931, two days after Reggie’s death, “I was at the auditorium of the high school watching a basketball game when a man came over the loudspeaker. He said news had been received that a large mob of angry Negroes from Kansas City and St. Joe were coming here with the intention of burning down the town and everyone in it. I was knocked over and stepped on when the auditorium emptied in about thirty seconds."

On her way home with her mother, she saw several groups of men storm several local businesses, taking every gun, ammunition, and weapon they could find and heading south of town to meet the 'black vigilantes'. This time, the guard unit at the armory was called, and for two days, the county held its breath, watchfully waiting, and prepared for another civil war battle. Left-over World War I cannons and machine guns were commanding the highest hill south of town and every other street intersection. The 'black' mob never arrived, and again, not a shot was fired.

Grandma gave birth to my mother on Jan. 18, 1931. In one conversation with my grandparents over a modest Sunday dinner while I was in graduate school, I explained I was doing a term paper on mob violence/lynching behavior and I wanted to know what had happened to create such a travesty of justice.

Reluctantly, they admitted granddad had played baseball with Reggie on occasion when an all 'white' local team would play an all 'black' team in an exhibition game. According to granddad, the 'white' team always won. While not knowing Thelma, Granddad revealed while standing outside the Carrott Schoolhouse, he heard Reggie confess just before it was ignited. Granddad had no doubt as to Reggie's guilt.

"The confession of a dying or about-to-die man should be taken as the gospel," he said.

"Any man will confess to anything if tortured enough," Grandma said. Granddad took his dishes to the kitchen without comment but I suspected he was listening just around the kitchen doorway.

She related Reggie was in the habit of stopping at the back door of their family home to pick up the local newspaper after the family had finished with it. He would take it to his home several blocks east on 4th St., where he lived on the other side of the tracks with his folks. She couldn't remember ever actually having a conversation with him.

On Thursday, December 18, 1930, after supposedly returning from the fields hunting, Reggie, reading about Thelma's murder in the newspaper, stated to grandma, "They'll accuse me of that," turned and walked toward his home.

Grandma said it was the most words at one time she ever heard him speak, and just about every time she ever saw him, he was with his mother, father, or older member of the Gumm family.

I questioned her further on details of Reggie's family, history, and lifestyle when granddad came back into the room. Knowing political arguments don't flavor a meal, she gently changed the subject and whispered, "I'll tell you later."

This was a favorite tactic whenever she suspected the subject wasn't appropriate for the current company.

Taking time out from her embroidery that afternoon, while granddad had gone to town for groceries, she recollected Reggie's mother, Bea Gumm, a medium height, heavy-set African-American woman, about 45 years of age at the time of the 'Burning', did housekeeping, odd jobs, as well as gardening, to help make ends meet.

She thought she remembered his father, Em, as disabled in a farming accident and unable to work with the exception of menial jobs around town but she was uncertain. I would later hear an unconfirmed rumor that he was injured when a 'still' blew up, along with several other 'bootleggers' in a turf war. She thought Reggie had been in trouble with the law before, but was unsure.

He appeared to be about 5 and a half feet tall, weighing about 125 lbs., a little slow in mental faculties, a thin physique, and walked with a loping gait. He appeared young for his age but otherwise physically normal for his mid-twenties, very dark complexion, short kinky black hair, clean-shaven, dark brown-eyed male, with the exception of a 'cauliflower' right ear. I told her she would have made a good cop from her description after all that time.

She stated she knew nothing personally about Reggie or his family other than to recognize them passing on the streets, as they kept to themselves. Other neighbors, while denying they knew Reggie or the Gumm family personally, confirmed what grandma told be. They all felt he might have been 'addled in the brain', to use their expression.

I didn't question them anymore that day and went back to my library search. The following weekend, we went to Marie and Gary's for Sunday dinner. They had since moved to Purington a few years after Mickey died. While Marie was showing me her garden, I told her what granddad and grandma told me about Reggie and Thelma. I reminded her of what she told me many years before in the henhouse but she couldn't remember much about the incident.

After 'hem-hawing' around for a few minutes, she finally stated she was about twenty-six years old and married to Gary at the time. A medium height, slender, attractive young woman with auburn hair and blue eyes, she had been a teacher in a rural school for about 7 years when news of Thelma's death struck terror in the hearts and souls of everyone.

She couldn't remember at any time, having actually met or seen Thelma or Reggie in person. She remembered that when asked, Gary provided leaders of the mob with a bull chain in preparation for the lynching and claimed to still have a link to it as a souvenir. When she went to find it in a corner windowsill on the back sun porch, it was gone.

She recalled the school principal on the day of the lynching, coming around to all the teachers saying, "They got that nigger!" which seemed to make everyone feel relieved. "Even so," she said, "no one but the law and the Good Lord are supposed to know when any of us are to die."

I asked her if she knew where Thelma was buried. It was reported in newspapers Thelma had been buried in Clermont, M.O., near where she was born, but my extensive research into the local graveyards failed to locate her grave. "Yes, I can take you right to it," she said.

"You can't have a murder without a body," I said.

"Get in the car," she replied.

Driving into Clermont, Aunt Marie said, "Just keep going," as we eventually came to the other side of town. Continuing to drive across the state line, I said, "Aunt Marlene, we're in Iowa."

A few miles later, we came to Clarenda, IA. At the city limits, I saw a cemetery and she asked me to stop. A few paces from the car, she stood over the graves of the Holster family. “Why is Thelma buried in Clarenda?” I asked.

“Don’t believe everything you read in the papers,” she replied.

After taking several pictures of the grave markers and cemetery, we went back home. I was never able to find anyone alive who admitted they actually knew Thelma during her short life. I did interview some of Thelma’s extended family members: Harold, Elza, and Barbara Holster, second cousins, who were born shortly before and after Thelma had died. They knew little about her, other than what other family members had told them and learned from family album photographs.

At the time of her death, she had three living older siblings: Orville, Letha, and Enis. It was revealed that as a child she had been rather sickly and treated for scoliosis of the spine with a long narrow metal rod in her back. It gave her the appearance of always looking at a slight angle toward whom or whatever she would focus her attention on.

Confirmed by photos they shared with me which suggested a happy childhood, she was the fifth of five children born to her biological, fairly ‘well-to-do’, farming parents and sometimes would become remorseful about her oldest brother, Floyd, who died in France during World War I.

Otherwise healthy at the time of her death, according to them, she had always been a very prim, proper, modestly attractive, and respectful daughter, student, and teacher. Standing about four feet-ten inches tall, weighing about 80 lbs. sopping wet, she had a flair for fashion but was never boastful, and felt she wanted to make her mark in history as a teacher, unsatisfied with the prospect of being a happily married 'stay-at-home' farmer's wife. She considered herself progressive and thought teaching evolution in public schools was her duty for a 'well-rounded' education.

I never successfully interviewed anyone who admitted actually knowing or being related to Reggie. Some county census records indicated the Gumm family had been rather large at one time and possibly of mixed racial parentage but no current known addresses were available.

According to government records, Reggie was the third of eleven children born to his parents, Em and Bea Gumm. Piecing together known habits and customs of the area, I believe he was born in a 'tent camp' on the banks of the 102 river, east of Berryville.

A name search of Ted Gumm, identified as one of Reggie's brothers in the newspapers but not listed in census records, (possibly an uncle/brother of Em), indicated he had possibly died under 'unexplained suspicious' hunting accident circumstances in 1932 in Kansas. Several years ago, a name search for Paul 'Shike' Smith, possibly an uncle by marriage and known hunting companion of Reggie's, revealed no records at all, as if he never existed.

Years later, after granddad's funeral, grandma finally told me a piece of the story which had been apparently known to the sheriff and Mickey but had remained unknown to the general public. Promising Momo, and granddad, never to repeat what she had seen or heard about the case, she would eventually answer some previously unanswered questions and raise some more. After grandma's funeral, Aunt Marlene would tell me even more that might have saved Reggie from the gallows, but not likely.

The Aftermath

A bell of injustice rang across the entire country and the world with the news of Reggie's death at the hands of 'white' vigilantes in the promised land of Nowadays County. Religious and political leaders in the country proclaimed 'two wrongs don't make a right'.

Since the incident occurred outside the 'Lynch Belt' of the south was so blatantly pre-planned and the actions of authorities were so obviously negligent in protecting an accused but 'innocent until found guilty in a court of law' defendant with National Guard troops stationed one block away intentionally deployed to prevent mob violence, the public-at-large outside the county demanded an undoing of many wrongs in the case.

But charges against those who caused the wrongful death of Reggie Gumm were never filed, nor were there any filed against others who might have been involved in Thelma's death. No one was talking, or just mysteriously disappeared for destinations unknown, or died under mysterious circumstances.

Unreported, unconfirmed, and unspeakable acts of violence were rumored to have subsequently been committed against 'blacks and whites' alike, both here in this country and abroad, when news of this incident circled the globe.

This incident was used as an example of what could happen in a corrupt capitalist society by dictators, communists, and fascists alike, trying to build a case against all forms of democratic governments. It was even necessary to quell disturbances/near riots in several major cities with government troops to avoid further bloodshed while testing our country's constitutional integrity in the process (Raper, 1989; Christensen, 1999; Time, 1931).

As a result of this episode in history, the legislature attempted to pass many laws that would prevent mob violence/lynching behavior from occurring again, without success.

Finally, about nine months after the Gumm incident, Governor Davis, under great pressure from many representatives of Kansas City and St. Louis, and many religious quarters around the state and nation, was able to successfully find a solution to the issue when he signed into law the formation of the Missouri State Highway Patrol, giving it full investigative, arrest, detention and prisoner protection authority.

It was believed this would make it nearly impossible for any person or mob to abduct a prisoner and cause bodily harm before, during, or after a trial. Time would prove he was right, as the number of confirmed 'lynchings' in Missouri dropped significantly, with the last confirmed one occurring in 1981 on Main St. of Slidemore, M.O., just a few miles southwest of where the Carrot School was located in Nowadays County (Frazier, 2009).

President Roosevelt, who ran on an anti-lynching plank in the Democratic Party National Platform, failed to sign legislation (Wagner-Costigan Act) outlawing mob violence, believing it was a states' rights issue but would create the Civil Rights Division of the United States Department of Justice within one year of taking office in 1933.

To say most of the people of Nowadays County were traumatized to the point of senseless revenge after hearing of Thelma's death would be an understatement. For the rest of their lives, all who lived in this area of the world during and after this time, scorn, ridicule, and ostracism would follow them to their dying days with many a soul carrying the memory of a burning man atop a schoolhouse, or the white shroud covering a lifeless young woman's body in a church while hundreds passed by to pay their respects.

Outside the county, almost no one had a kind word for those who took the law into their own hands, or those who stood by doing nothing; most just refused to make any comment at all. For every soul who heard or knew the story, there would always be plenty of false 'justification' for continued prejudice and racism against all their fellow Americans: Black, red, yellow, or white who didn't conform to time-honored codes and accepted standards of 'American' group behavior.

According to U.S. census records, Nowadays County was at an all-time high of 32,938 in 1900. In 1930, there were 26,371. The county census record for 1931 indicated the population was 27,774, suggesting a significant increase from the previous year but over the next several decades, this number gradually reduced to 22,215 by 1960.

The differences in population totals between county, state, and federal government records suggest someone may have been 'cooking the books' to claim a greater need for maintaining or expanding state and federal legislative representation and funding than there actually was. It was this practice that initially led to the formation of the Federal Census Bureau in the first place and wasn't an uncommon practice in most counties. Undoubtedly, over this time, more people were leaving than were coming in.

Of 90 African-American people who were living in the area at the time, about two-thirds left overnight when news of Reggie making his first confession 'leaked out'. The rest left when he was killed, with the exception of one black man and his small family. They were left unharmed due to the fact he had served in W.W. I and proved his commitment to our country's way of life. It wasn't until after W.W. II that a significant number of African-Americans returned to Nowadays County; most of them being veterans who had proved themselves 'worth of the trust' (Cooper, 1986).

Nevertheless, deep-seated bigotry and hatred between the races would permeate every relationship among all those living in the county for generations to come. In fact, the only time I ever saw Granddad get mad enough to strike anyone (I was 9 yrs. old) was when Aunt Pozzy announced in the front room that 'black kids' were seen at the public swimming pool the previous afternoon. Granddad proclaimed, "If they get in the pool, you all get out and come home!"

Pozzy started to protest when Grandma came out of the kitchen and informed her she would do as she was told. Indeed, we came home early and played quietly in the backyard sprinkler for the rest of the afternoon.

In those days, people took pride in their work and did the best they could with the best resources available. In order to achieve the best possible outcomes of their labors, there were numerous social subgroups promoting their own unique themes and agendas through religious, ancestral heritage off-shouts, political, occupational, educational, and even sexual identity exclusivity (i.e., Sons of Liberty, Odd Fellows, Eastern Star, Delphi Society, K.K.K., etc.).

When a threat was perceived, the bonds of the 'greater' group membership would be tightened with the need to overcome the threat, while subgroup bonds would be seemingly subservient for 'the good of the whole'.

The Motives

Could Reginald Gumm have been totally innocent of all charges in the death of Thelma Holster? Could he have just been a 'fall guy', made to order for the part with a prior criminal history of attacking a white student/teacher and being a little on the 'odd' side?

It is not likely, since he was found with bloodstains on him, as were his two hunting companions, a bite mark on his thumb, a bloodstained fingerprint at the crime scene on a piece of paper, and a boot print found near the scene matching his. The blood could have been rabbit blood from hunting, and many people could have left a similar boot print. But a bite mark match with the victims' dental structure and a bloodstained fingerprint, supposedly held by the coroner, would be impossible to falsify.

In his confession, he described the actions and scene of the crime which matched the physical evidence. According to authorities, he told them where they could find the murder weapon which he just picked up on the way to the schoolhouse and discarded on the way back to town. Could anyone else have done that?

Yes, if his confession was a total fabrication beaten out of him by authorities who knew where to find the murder weapon in the first place. And what of Thelma's jewelry, which was reported as missing but never reported as found?

He said he threw it away with the 'club' murder weapon. A knife sharp enough to inflict the lacerations on Thelma's body noted in the coroner's autopsy but never found, suggests both disorganized and organized killer personality characteristics in a crime of passion.

The motive(s) for Thelma's murder is (are) perplexing and virtually impossible to conceive. Could Reggie have confessed, at first, so as to protect others involved? Given his purported level of intellectual development, I'm inclined to think so.

What's perplexing, but telling, is the fact that bloodhounds went off in southerly but slightly different directions from the schoolhouse; except one trail, the shortest way back to town to the northeast, that Reggie described in his confession. Also, at first, there were no fingerprints publicly confirmed to be found at the crime scene. If he wore gloves to account for this fact, then how could he have had a serious bite mark on his thumb?

Assuming just about every white person, and many blacks in the county, were right in the suspicion that Reggie was guilty of killing Thelma, could he have done it alone, just for sadistic sexual self-gratification and aggrandizement motives in one of the most heinous, maniacal manners imaginable since 'Jack the Ripper', and leaving little traces of himself at the crime scene, with very little noticeable disruption of the physical environment except possibly one or two desks moved out of line, no signs of forced entry, no one hearing Thelma's screams for help, and in about an hour's time?

Could Reggie, and his companions, actually have acted in concert, committing the crime? This is more probable than not. I'm more inclined to believe this scenario than any other involving Reggie in Thelma's murder since his confession reads more like he was a passive part-time observer participant in the crime as opposed to the sole initiator of the criminal scenario.

His interchangeable use of first and third-person pronouns and verbiage contexts suggests this or may have been just his manner of sub-average intellectual functioning. It may also be the real reason the confession was not reprinted in the public media, which was a common practice for those times when it was available. The first time I requested to see the signed confession Reggie was purported to have made, I was shown what appeared to be a copy of the original document.

Some years later, when I wanted to recheck some facts from additional eyewitness testimony, I was told the document wasn't available.

There are many mixed 'organized and disorganized' features about the crime scene that suggest others could have been involved. The scene had all the 'ear-marks' of a crime of passion: premeditated, ritualistic, in a vengeful frantic homicidal mania process.

The 'organized' serial sexual offender is usually above average in the intelligence of a socialized-aggressive personality type, with a 'rape kit', much-advanced planning, escape plans including victim hiding, excessive interest in victim's identity/characteristics and removing clothing and personal items for non-materialistic or idiosyncratic reasons.

The 'disorganized' serial sexual 'offender' killer is usually below average in intelligence of a non-socialized-aggressive personality with little or no pre-planning, doesn't appear to have any logic in the picking of a victim, has little or no interest in identity or characteristics of the victim, leaves the victim in plain view, obtains weapons from just what might be available at the time in the general vicinity and may cut off parts of a victim's body. Both these types learn from crime to crime and appear to get better at their 'work' over time if not apprehended soon (Innes, 2005).

If Thelma's murder wasn't just a senseless act by a lone, deranged, possibly developmentally disabled African-American 'Moron', or a small group of conspirators, then who could have had the means, motive, and opportunity to have killed her in such a way as previously described? Who would have stood to gain the most from her death? What needs would her death have fulfilled? Could there have been a 'Murder LLC' faction?

Waiting for the highest bidder to employ them to eliminate a possible embarrassment to powerful others, or a witness to their criminal activity? Let's just speculate for a moment, shall we?

Unless there simply wasn't enough time for the perpetrator(s) to conceal the crime by removing the body, to leave her in plain view in the middle of an isolated but public place suggests something of an attempt to fulfill a disorganized deranged egocentric 'look at me'/attention-seeking goal, by someone of below intellectual development, who was used to getting a lot of negative punishing attention but wanted more positive rewards, and who had not been successful in their attempts, not at least recently. And the fact Thelma was found without any of her customary jewelry would suggest a simple theft motive.

The commission of Thelma's murder could have represented a display of inadequacy on the part of the murderer, intended to satisfy intra-personal needs of making up for past failure(s) in relationships with objects of affection. Usually intended to alleviate self-pity and sorrow feelings of guilt, the killer(s) usually leave some sort of a subtle message at the crime scene which doesn't always make much sense upon initial investigation but reveals symbolic clues to the crime's solution, (i.e., three wise owls, three wise men, three slash marks by her ear).

Thelma's murder could have represented a power and control goal fulfillment process. This may have been the killer's (s) first successful attempt. Or, it could have been just one in a long series of similar incidents in other locales that made the killer feel it was necessary to resort to expanding their territorial hunting grounds, in order to achieve the 'sexual thrill' and escape apprehension. This is usually noted in the disabling of the victim by mechanical devices such as ropes, chains, gauges, etc., but with a higher level of intellectual development than was ever apparently achieved by Reggie.

Revenge goals may have been motivating the killer(s) to fulfill a 'getting even' need, not necessarily with dramatic punishment of response-cost strategies, but not beyond those possibilities, and could include signs of extreme degradation. Nudity, bondage, multiple stab wounds, and sexual assault suggest the death of Thelma could have been an attempt to fulfill this type of goal, only magnified a hundred times over.

Considering the manner in which she met her horrendous demise and the lack of much in the way of identified physical evidence, one would have to conclude a deceitful intellect was at work, with multiple costumes and disguises utilized.

Serial sexual criminals are not ordinarily born psychopaths but rather develop over years of systematic verbal and physical abuse and neglect with an aberrant internalized value/belief system.

In their childhoods and adolescence, if they live that long, they are usually identified as having 'difficulty' learning in traditional educational settings, and their peer group usually spares, then no form of hard-heartedness. Significant others expose them to promiscuous or graphic adult negative role models from an early age, usually of a sexual nature. Thus, by the time they are expected to assume adult roles, they are neither prepared nor welcome the opportunity to take on the responsibilities of socially mature adulthood.

The adult socialized perpetrator is usually first a child or adolescent voyeur in their early development. They tend to find accomplices to victimize who are more likely younger 'people pleasing' personality types of similar socio-cultural backgrounds; naïve, trusting, and not expecting compromising situations the perpetrator arranges for them.

Over time, the adolescent perpetrator may molest younger children and find more and more creative ways of intimidating victims into silence with the threat the victim will be exposed to authorities for past embarrassing or compromising code of conduct and behavior; perpetuating a psycho-sexual traumatizing sequential process with the victim.

When the threats no long have the desired effect on the victim, the perpetrator either eliminates the victim in ways that leave no trace where possible, or leaves the victim free to do what they will; hoping they will remain silent. If the victim threatens the perpetrator with exposure to authorities, they will have sealed their own doom, unless the victim is seen by the perpetrator as making the world more interesting with them in it, or the victim is a 'blood'/family relation, as in the case of incest.

While expecting all the privileges a right of a person with full citizenship and none of the responsibilities, and imagined social maturity in the internalized fantasy world of their own mind, they misperceive judgment by God, whom they think they are an instrument of, in most cases, or may even blame God for all their misfortunes and just want to see the world burn.

Unrelenting resentment, teasing, bullying, and forcing the individual to perform sexual or sadistic behaviors toward just about any living creature can, over time, result in aberrant personality formation, like the one necessary to have committed the murder of Thelma Holster, and may even cause anatomical changes in the brain with prolonged bio-chemical imbalances.

Most likely starting with a physical deformity of a prominent or clearly visible part of the body, leading to a disruption in identity formation and/or body dysmorphic disorder, the developing perpetrator experiences their first intimate relationship with a member of the opposite sex with disastrous effects, up to and including rejection, ridicule, physical assault and/or sexually transmitted disease(s). (Bigger is not always better, as many Marfane syndrome patients can attest to, and too small can have its embarrassing moments as well, as many Klinefelter syndrome patients can attest until they meet a woman with vaginismus).

A dissociation trance disorder may also be present, especially if they were raised in a culture where living sacrifices were part of the religious rituals of the dominant group or class. The disrupted integrative functions of memory, identity, and/or consciousness, or the conviction of having been taken over by a spirit, a deity, or another person may be present during a 'trance-like state'/phase of the disorder.

Interictal behavior syndrome (temporal lobe epileptic personality), as well as intermittent explosive disorder, would also have to be considered as differential diagnoses for ruling in or out upon neuro-psychiatric examination.

When the child (4-6 yrs. old) fails to desexualize the relationship of both parents or significant others and doesn't retain affectionate kinship with both of them, the normal internalization process is arrested, with the images of both parents having a negative effect on shaping the child's personality with an aberrant value system that rarely, if ever, achieves complete adult social maturity.

Eventually, the child's biological drives, interacting with the environment, leads to unbalanced reality-orientation development with dispute fixation and conflict ensuing (i.e., psycho-viscosity). Cognitive dissonance results from the individual's inability to rationalize the resulting friction between their aberrant internal value/belief system and the reality of external phenomena which does not fit or match the internal world of the child/individual.

This results in almost every experience the individual has been attributed to external factors seemingly beyond the control of the individual, or their own negative attributes. In reaction to enduring severe psycho-viscosity, personality disorders of just about every kind, especially those of an anti-social nature, and associated symptoms, as well as numerous disruptive behavior disorders of varying degrees of severity, duration, frequency, and intensity (acting-out episodes) and delusional-manic episodes are born.

Later on at subsequent stages of psycho-sexual development, they go beyond the figurative ingestion of a psychic representation of a person, or parts of the person, to a literal phase which is then labeled psychotic cannibalism, when they believe they have achieved mythic 'incorporation' of the valued or devalued external object(s) of their attentions, for whatever distorted coveting need they are driven to fulfill.

They then continue to go through life with much fear and hatred of others, especially members of the opposite sex, consciously, and themselves, subconsciously. Failing with just about every attempt at a serious relationship with another person, hoping it will all end with at least one final gratifying thrill before their own death which to them would be better than continuing to go on living the way they are.

They continue their quest for victims of opportunity, and when it is all over, immediately after the victim's death and their own 'psycho-orgasmic thrill' with a rush of hormone-based euphoria, usually with blood on their hands, they have a moment of clarity. Realizing the fuller implications of their actions and need to escape the immediate situation in order to avoid contact with authorities and continue their 'life of crime', they are most likely to make a mistake and leave tell-tale signs of their dastardly deed(s) in patterns that they may be only vaguely aware of, if at all.

Ordinarily, they neither readily extend themselves to others, nor readily accept others unless it is to take advantage of some material or self-gratifying way, thinking they are risking little or nothing at the time. Systematized delusional belief patterns, and possible dissociative trance characteristics, are common in these individuals with themes of grandiosity, paranoia, and jealousy noticeably present, all wrapped up into one personality and very resistant to treatment or amelioration, if not impossible to treat.

In extreme cases, the interactive sensory hallucinatory activity of all sensory modalities may also be present. Their daily schedules are inconsistent and irregular. They live in non-descript generic outwardly looking abodes for the neighborhood they occupy; usually alone or with an elderly relative they cling to for financial support. Inside their homes, it looks like a pack of rats has been living there; blending in outwardly, while chaotic on the inside.

A complete developmental history, indicating seizure-like activity within the first 36 months of life, or severe traumatic brain injury without proper treatment, may reveal the basis for serial psychopathic killer personality growth in conjunction with punishing and neglectful social learning history.

They appear to also be prone to bowel and bladder accidents past the age of 5, suggesting a heightened arousal potential for tactile sexual stimulation (e.g., easily stimulated), disrupted biofeedback-loop/brain circuitry and later may display paraphilias with premature puberty onset, and difficulties in transition phases of psycho-sexual development, ages 9-12.

As they grow older, they may feel compelled to search out pornographic materials and prostitutes or exotic entertainers for diversions, if not sadistic need fulfillment. Also, highly suggestible with noticeable susceptibility to hypnosis, altered consciousness, and responsiveness to external stimuli are markedly diminished or selectively focused with amnesic episodes possibly noted.

If more than one person was involved in Thelma's murder, it was probably someone who previously knew either Thelma or Reggie, or both, in the guise of an influential and respected member of the prevailing dominant social order, of superior and cunning self-serving intellectual development, organized with pre-planning in finding ways to approach both and win their confidence, manipulating underlings to take care of all the details, leaving no loose ends and/or 'dirty work', and possibly not even present at the time of the crime.

The 'mastermind' would promise some sort of reward as a commission for committing the crime, or avoidance of negative consequences, such as a threat to harm the underling or loved ones in order to gain their cooperation in the plot.

The 'mastermind' (Murder LLC) scenario would also require the underlings to be either protected for future use or eliminated in such a way as not to reveal who was pulling the strings of the plot.

Besides the usual characteristics noted in most psychopathic killer profiles, they would only feel remorse for themselves if caught while not displaying any signs of the personality traits which reveal who they really are; absent effect, or masking sympathy/empathy. They fixate on anyone they perceive as related or similar to the negative social stimuli they have a negative psycho-social learning history with, or have been paid to the target.

Today, they would probably have an emergency scanner to track the movements of authorities or know someone on the inside of the local power structure who would give them a 'heads up' on the movement of authorities. And they would usually be financially well off enough to be able to afford the necessary payoffs, tools, and equipment of their trade, escape mechanisms, and concealing locations.

Socialized types may often appear very flamboyant, outgoing, and personable in social contexts which they usually avoid as they get older, while distant, secretive, or manipulative in isolated one-on-one interactions with those they feel are of inferior caliber, beyond a simple quasi-socialized but devious aggressive anti-social personality disorder or Borderline Personality Disorder. They follow predatory criminal pursuits with compulsive, addictive, and poor impulse control personality disorder signs and symptoms.

The childhood development of an unbalanced internalization/externalization process, possibly with a genetic predisposition for negative temperament, creates the need to transform from what the serial killer unconsciously believes they are; a less than entirely desirable human being. With ‘super persona’, they mistakenly believe they will transform into the ‘hero’ of humanity that they never became and never will.

Most serial killers keep some sort of trophy/item from their victim(s) to gloat over and be reminded of the exhilaration, up to and including eating body parts (psychotic introjections), so as to fulfill an aberrant internalization goal(s).

When confronted with evidence of their crime, they elaborately rationalize and justify their own behavior with alibis and distractions to blame others who must be of subnormal intellectual development or social maturity. They will use general terms to suggest one direction of intent, while actually concealing the truth of their actions; saying they went ‘abroad’, which commonly meant going east, while actually going west.

The killer covets the things they believe are virtuous, honorable, and desirable, but unable to obtain through socially accepted means. They erroneously think their actions will get them what they want, which is psychotic self-actualization, and if the victim is punished or dies, the killer will never feel harmed or offended again by them, or others like them. Proving themselves superior to all others, the killers’ unbalanced internal judge vacillates with decisions about who would best be left in the world, and who the world would be better off without.

When the object of their momentary affection reacts negatively, it starts a chain reaction of escalating violence which will silence the victim and keep the killer from being exposed to negative reactions of the victim. Misperceiving the victim and all others like them to appear to finally accept the killer, they may keep a lifeless victim as the only possible proof of the killer's 'superiority' and their guilt.

Psycho-viscosity in a systematized delusional belief pattern forces the killer to feel panic and start to initiate the escape phase of the criminal scenario. Accelerated thinking and speaking, flight of ideas, hyperactivity, excessive elation (euphoria) or irritability (dysphoria), inflated self-image, and grandiosity are characteristics of the Bi-Polar roller coaster these individuals find themselves living on, by their own devices.

Over time, if they successfully escape apprehension, they can become addicted to the short-term gratification(s)/thrill(s) and unable to resist the temptation of killing again to enjoy the aberrant sensations, and usually kill more frequently due to a 'diminishing return' effect with each subsequent murder,(stimulus habituation), and rarely if ever display stimulus satiation, or 'getting enough'. The first incident will probably occur closest to where the killer lives or works with later crimes committed further and further away as they extend their area of operations in search of new victims to rid the world of.

Usually only being stopped by legal authorities, their own death by their own hand, the hands of the victim(s) who actually are able to defend themselves, and underlings too, they will meet their final unnatural end, eventually. The latter two scenarios are of relatively low probability. The memory of committing the crime is insufficient to maintain the accompanying exhilaration the perpetrator feels with the original act of committing the crime.

A mob/crowd taking souvenirs from a crime scene they have actively or inactively participated in represents the groups' attempt to restore the unbalanced collective internalization process they experienced after the initial 'trigger'. While gaining physical evidence of their deed, they will be reminded of the original incident and its short-term gratification, indelibly imprinted in their collective memory and social learning schema to vicariously relive the episode, reminding them of the transformed 'criminal act' and its' justification.

Thus, racial, religious, sexist, and other prejudices and addictions are perpetuated in the human experience down through subsequent generations by genetic predispositions, negative role models, group rules of conduct, prohibitions, warnings, and cautions with or without factual or rational evidence to fully substantiate them, including the material souvenirs of the incident. They reinforce the notion that past behavior is the best predictor of future behavior, taken on faith because if it happened once, it could happen again. Besides, it might be worth something someday.

Could Thelma have had incriminating information or evidence about somebody that motivated them to eliminate her in such a way that would conceal the information/evidence and cast blame on someone else? Several bootlegging, gambling, and prostitution operations were rumored to have been in existence at the time she might have stumbled on too. Other criminal acts could have been taking place while the 'mastermind' and everyone in town were tromping over the Carrott School grounds, but none were reported.

Making a mess of the crime scene, supposedly trying to solve Thelma's murder, making themselves the 'hero' of the group, and diverting attention and resources from other criminal acts could be a ploy of a 'mastermind' who will often return to the scene of the crime to determine what else they need to do to conceal their own culpability in the crime. Socialized group psychopathic killers will leave evidence in multiple false trails to deceive those who are hunting them; usually in opposite directions, all except the 'fall guy' of the group, who usually is elected to take the most obvious and shortest route to supposed safety.

To commit the murder of Thelma Holster by parties unknown and to leave as little trace evidence as possible in the schoolhouse, suggests Thelma may have been killed in one of the other buildings, or vehicle, and then moved to the schoolhouse center floor, amounting to a 'staging' of the scene.

Considering the amount of time the scene was left unattended between when the last pupil left, August leaving when his sister called him home and Thelma's landlord returning with a relative, could there have been someone concealing themselves on school grounds, waiting for their chance to escape? Possibly, but who of even below-average intelligence would leave a bloodstained fingerprint on plain paper at the crime scene, knowing authorities had their prints on file from a previous arrest?

Could a jealous lover, or female competitor for the attentions of a mutual lover, knowing she was pregnant with his child, who felt betrayed when she started seeing another man or just broke off the relationship, be so jealous it drove them to perform such an act? There is only about a 50/50 chance of this being the case, but only when there is circumstantial evidence or testimony confirming part or all of the scenario, and would require a modern forensic autopsy of 'Thelma' remains to confirm her pregnancy, extent of wounds and presences of toxic substances or others' DNA.

Also, if news was circulated that she had been seen keeping company with several different men and was sexually active, whether true or not, it could have been taken as an embarrassment to many authority figures, some of whom may have been in a supervisory capacity.

Could a former or current student, or their family member, feel they had been so mistreated by an uppity new first-year teacher that they retaliate in such a vicious manner; not necessarily intending to go as far as they did, but wouldn't back down when push came to shove?

Not likely, though not impossible, even if she contended the student could not be educated through accepted educational methods of the day, they could always go to work in a vocation of their choosing suited to their skills and aptitude levels. It is curious that the school had only five students attending classes at the time. How could this be when the population of the county was still relatively large?

Could a disgruntled qualified teacher who didn't get the job Thelma was given at one of the oldest and most prestigious examples of the 'one-room-schoolhouse' in the country, thinking they would be next in line if Thelma was scared off or eliminated, be involved? Even less likely, though not impossible, this scenario would have to be considered a low probability with multiple motives in play, even as desperate as most people were at the time because you could always get another job. Couldn't you?

Could the original landowner, or their survivors, where the school was located, expect to regain possession of it at a time when the land was the only thing that lasted and was worth fighting for, or even worth dying for? It would take a very power/control motivated but misguided 'mastermind' to implement a criminal plan such as the one which resulted in Thelma's death. Pursuing this sort of goal, and not being a likely suspect, is virtually impossible to escape the attention of authorities unless they had a 'go between' middleman, who was acting under orders and sworn to secrecy by the threat of retaliation.

Could one of Thelma's family members, or others, stand to gain an inheritance benefit from her death: insurance, will, entailment, trust, or the like? Nothing in my research suggests this to be the case, but it is not outside the realm of human possibilities. Could Reggie's first 'attempted' rape victim or her family have been involved, seeking revenge and setting him up, seeing to it he got what they thought he deserved the first time? Not likely without multiple motives in play, but possible.

Was the sheriff as much of a 'buffoon' as he was made out to be in the regional and national press? I don't think so. He knew he was in over his head, to begin with, and called for help. Several mistakes were made but when discovered, they tried to correct them the best they could with the resources they had available at the time.

Did he feel any guilt or responsibility for the death of Thelma due to not taking her pleas for help as seriously as he could have? I imagine so. Or was he in on a plot that ultimately led to Thelma's and Reggie's deaths? Not likely. Could he have been intentionally misled by community members to believe Reggie would get a fair trial with no need to call out the National Guard? I'm inclined to believe so.

Could the discovery of 'bloody underwear' actually have been a significant clue in the case, but was never fully followed up, or in fact covered up? Yes, but without a chain of evidence procedure and forensic laboratory examination for comparison to the blood of both Reggie and Thelma, it may have been less convincing to a jury. The fact it was found near a junction of two of the three major railroads in the county could suggest an escape path for the killer(s).

Who were the most influential members of the community, and were they advocating law and order, or anarchy? By most accounts, they were on the side of law and order. Could they have been misled by supremacist groups who had infiltrated the county's social and political power structures? Yes, it is a distinct possibility.

If I had been investigating the case at the time, I would have rounded up all the known criminals within a 100 miles radius of the Carrott Schoolhouse and determined which ones didn't have an air-tight alibi; searching highways, trains, rivers, aircraft, and any other possible mode of transportation, matching M.O. histories with the currently known facts. Clearly, it may be just idle speculation at this point since the passage of time and the destruction of the crime scene makes complete identification of the case impossible. The importance of accurate and speedy analysis of details large and small can't be understated.

Unless the law and its due processes are allowed to proceed, there is virtually no way of knowing the whole truth and thus administering justice to all truly guilty parties, while setting the innocent free. Even at that time, magistrates said it was better that 99 guilty parties go free than one innocent person be found guilty and punished for a crime they didn't commit.

Normally, when a person commits a premeditated volitional act, they have already determined its compliance with accepted group norms and rules of conduct. If the act was determined to be out of compliance with group codes of conduct, it was displayed for selfish reasons to begin with and the individual was punishable by law. In all criminal acts, the known risk(s) are minimized and perceived as worth the inflated selfish reward(s).

For academics and research enthusiasts, Miller and Dollard (1939) still present the best psycho-social behavioral analysis/profile of mob/lynching behavior to date, as it did when I completed my term paper in 1978 for my class in 'The Psychology of Group Behavior'. Leon Festinger's Theory of Cognitive Dissonance (1957) expanded to a social group analysis does help explain how the collective conscience of a group can follow an erroneous path of irrational ideas to an absurd unlawful conclusion.

The best way of dealing with mobs is explained in the story of Wyatt Earp's defense of Tommy O'Rourke in 1878(?).

Sister's Secrets

About a month after Granddad's funeral, one Saturday evening in June 1994, I was sitting in the front room of Grandma's house with her watching her favorite television program, 'The Grand Old Opry'. She had always wished she could attend in person. I told her I had decided to write a story about Thelma and Reggie, and I wanted her to tell me the rest of what she had left out so many years before.

"Why do you want to drag all that up now?" she asked as she turned down her TV with her remote.

"Others can learn from the tragedy of Thelma and Reggie, and maybe something like that might never happen again," I replied.

She finally relented saying, "Well, I guess now that your granddad is dead, it doesn't make any difference." Granddad died as the result of falling twenty feet off the roof of his house at the age of 87 while trying to trim back some tree limbs, with Grandma holding the ladder. He wanted to save the money and do it himself.

She said on the morning of December 21, 1930, a frigid but sunny day, Mrs. Bea Gumm came to the back door of their house and asked if it was alright to place a burlap sack of flower buds in the root cellar. Mrs. Gumm said she had already talked to Momo and had gotten permission to do so when she was ready to store them for the winter. A musty scent rose from the cellar as Grandma watched Mrs. Gumm place the sack in the root cellar, close the door, and wave goodbye as she turned to walk home.

When Momo got back, Grandma told her Mrs. Gumm had been there. Momo said she didn't know anything about any flower bulbs and went to get the sheriff, telling Grandma to stay in the house and lock the door until Momo returned. They returned to the house about a half-hour later and Grandma saw the sheriff remove the sack from the cellar. When he emptied the sack on the ground, there among the flower bulbs was a watch, necklace, ring, bracelet, and a set of Christmas-decorated earrings. Later, Thelma's mother and father would identify them as belonging to Thelma.

Suddenly, I realized some references to her watch never being found in the search for Thelma's murderer and no mention of a knife being found which was supposedly the instrument used to inflict three slashes on her neck behind her ear, as well as other injuries. Up until then, nothing about the case history had suggested theft as a motive.

"Grandma, do you realize what you're saying?" I questioned.

"Yes. And if called to testify, I'll tell the same story the same way because that's what happened." She was adamant.

"Was a knife in the sack?" I quarried.

"Not that I saw," she replied.

"Do you realize how it might look in court?" I asked. She didn't say anything; just looked down at the floor with her thumbnail between her front teeth, which she always did when trying to remember something deep in thought.

"What became of the jewelry?" I asked.

"The last time I saw it, it was in the hands of the sheriff. He and Momo were walking toward the Gumm house," she said.

At the time this happened, Reggie was in custody in the Buchcannon County Jail in St. Joe. Naturally, I asked, "Do you think Mrs. Gumm knew the jewelry was in that sack?"

She replied, "No, I don't think so. She didn't seem nervous, upset, or anything. I just don't know."

Momo told Grandma the sheriff confronted Mrs. Gumm with the sack. Denying any idea the jewelry was in it, she pleaded with the sheriff to see her 'touched' son got a fair trial, saying, "There's something not right with that boy!"

For days before and after Thelma's killing, Reggie had not been himself. Even so, just about anyone could have placed the jewelry in the sack, as Reggie was in custody at the time, and the flower bulbs had supposedly been under the Gumms' back porch since October.

Mrs. Gumm felt 'Shike' Smith, Reggie's uncle by marriage and hunting companion, could have led him into trouble as Reggie didn't have sense enough to stalk a victim, plan ahead with a weapon and not leave a trace. Seasoned, trained bloodhounds won't lose the scent of someone covered in blood for no good reason, either. The sheriff, Momo, and Granddad admonished Grandma never to discuss the case with anyone unless she was called to testify in court under oath.

When I was first reviewing the indictment records of three cases Reggie had been involved with in Nowadays County Circuit Court, I observed the name of Mrs. Bea Gumm as item eleven on a nineteen-item list of state witnesses attached to the indictment papers provided to me by a Deputy Circuit Court Clerk. I thought at the time I reviewed the list, it was unusual for one of Reggie's family members to be called to testify for the state unless they were going to be treated as a hostile witness, to begin with. Momo and Grandma were not listed.

"It says in the Bible that the wicked flee when no one chases them, but you must never mistreat a person, or stand by and let another do so. Having the courage to do what is right; this is the true meaning of honor. It develops in a person over time after they have been tested by life and speaks to all others without having to say a word. There was no honor in what was done to Reggie or Thelma, and I'm ashamed to admit, I didn't have the courage to stand up to that cowardly mob. Instead, I stayed at home, thinking I was going to have a baby, your mother, any day," Grandma said.

"Now, you have my final word on it. If you think you can write a book so something like that never happens again, you do that now," she said softly with a trembling voice.

I said I would, as she turned up the volume on her TV. We never spoke about the incident again, except once when I told her I hoped Granddad had asked forgiveness for whatever role he might have played in the 'burning' incident before he passed away. After all, if Grandma's boy can't believe his own Grandma, who can he believe?

The next morning after we ate breakfast, cleared away, and washed all the dishes, we were sitting at the dining room table considering what the daily agenda would include.

"Rodger, what am I going to do with all of this stuff?" she asked.

"What stuff?" I asked.

"All of Granddad's stuff he left here in the house, under the house, in the attic, and in the garage? There must be a ton of it," she replied.

I thought about it a minute and said, "We can go through every item and determine if it ought to be kept, sold in a yard sale, given away, or thrown away. Do you want to start at the top and work down, or start at the bottom and work our way up?"

She didn't cherish the idea of climbing up two flights of stairs to a dusty attic, so we started in the basement.

There was every kind of old carpentry tools, pieces of lumber, furniture repair and painting supplies, brushes, cabinets full of old buckets partially filled with paint/varnish, old empty and full bottles of Coca-Cola crates, work clothes, dress clothes, and rags.

Fishing tackle and poles, one old Ithaca shotgun with several boxes of shells, books and magazines mostly about the great outdoors/naturalist themes, and tons of photographs/ memorabilia from his youth and previous generations in the family that had been handed down from his parents and their parents, and so on, until the items finally ended up in one nook or cranny of my grandparents' house.

Each item received her attention and disposition declaration in a 'matter-of-fact' manner, just as if she knew what Granddad would have done with it if he had been there himself, seemingly without any regrets. After going thru four floors of the house, I remembered there was a closet on the back porch we hadn't tackled. I said, "Wait a minute Grandma, we haven't looked into the closet on the back porch."

She said, "Oh yes, I forgot about that one."

As we stood in front of the closet, I pulled back one of its sliding doors that Granddad had built when they first moved into the place and found more hanging work clothes, boots, and more fishing tackle. After clearing away some items on top, I notice I don't know how many bottles of just about every kind of old whiskey, and assorted liquor containers you could imagine. Since I had never seen Granddad or Grandma take a drink in my life, I asked, "Why are there so many liquor bottles in here?"

"Granddad liked to entertain company when they would come by," she said.

I told her I didn't know what she wanted to do with the material items, but there would be no need to keep the liquid beverages. She agreed, and I dumped all the bottles in the kitchen sink and threw them away; enough to fill an entire garbage can.

As we worked our way thru the hanging clothes items, covered with multiple layers of cobwebs and dust, I came to an old woolen scarlet red hunting coat that wasn't entirely red. It had black checked lines crossing each other in a design reminiscent of a Scottish Highlands Clan. I asked, "What do you want to do with this?"

"Burn it! Just take it out and burn it!" she said without hesitation. I started to argue it looked like it could be cleaned and given away to the poor for the winter, or maybe given to someone else in the family, or sold in a yard sale maybe. She finally said, "I don't care what you do with it."

Apologetically, I hung it back where it was, to begin with, and didn't mention it again, as it was the only thing in the house that appeared to have caused any kind of emotional reaction in her. After dry-cleaning it, she stated she would give it to her youngest grandson, but I'm not sure what became of it, as the house was sold after her funeral six years later.

Grandma passed away at the age of 87 years young from a fall in her bathtub. Later, at the hospital, we would say our last goodbye when I kissed my fingertips and placed them on her forehead. After the funeral service, the minister told me he had never seen two sisters-in-law as close as Grandma and Aunt Marie were. It was as if they were a 'blood' relation. She and her secret finally belonged to the ages, or so I thought.

By this time, great Aunt Marie was in an assisted-living facility, nine months short of her 99th birthday. As luck would have it, I was passing thru the area on my way home and I went to share dinner with her. After reviewing a lot of 'water under the bridge', I told her about all the research I had done on the killing of Thelma and Reggie and wanted to know if she might be able to shed any more light on the subject. For instance, how did she know Thelma's grave was in Iowa and why was Thelma's grave in Iowa? Where was her jewelry? And who did she think actually killed Thelma and Reggie?

"Rodger, you just won't let this go, will you?" she asked.

"Not likely," I replied.

"I think I've lived too long," she said as she sat down in her rocking chair.

"Why do you say that?" I asked.

She stated she missed all the people she had known, loved, and cared for over her lifetime and wondered if she would ever see all of them again in heaven. Gently redirecting her back to the subject, I told her I thought all people could learn a valuable lesson from the story of these two people if they had all the facts.

"After they burned Reggie on top of the old Carrott Schoolhouse and burned down the Gumm residence, there were a lot of upset people who questioned whether Reggie was guilty of killing Thelma at all, or acted alone, not to mention the mockery they made of our nation's justice system," she said.

I sat quietly, open-mouthed for about two hours as she related how many government and private investigators from all over the country turned the county upside down, trying to find evidence in the case that would show what the truth was. But no one was talking, out of fear of reprisals from both whites and blacks, not to mention all the wrongful death suits that could be brought against the city and county officials.

She related how unknown parties had desecrated Thelma's grave in Clermont and chastised the Holster family for instigating the riotous behavior of the mob that denied Reggie a fair trial, destroyed public and private property, as well as the good name of the people who lived in the county.

"Mickey and the sheriff were livid and felt betrayed!" she said, as they had been promised by leaders and members of the community there would be no unlawful reprisals or anarchy. In fact, Mickey was at a cattle sale in St. Joe at the time. Even local residents and longtime friends of the Holster family turned on them to the point they finally left the county and the state for 'parts unknown' to the general public.

"It was good old Uncle Harry, who gave the family Thelma's jewelry after Reggie was killed. The jewelry was buried with Thelma when she was subsequently moved to the cemetery in Clarinda, where the Holster family had relocated," she said.

"Do you know why the mob from Kansas City never came as it had been rumored?" I asked.

"It was good old Uncle Harry and Bea Gumm who met with leaders of the black mob in St. Joe and told them how Thelma's jewelry was found and that they believed Reggie had been involved in the crime but felt he did not act alone. They convinced the 'black' mob that those responsible for both Thelma and Reggie dying would be brought to justice, no matter how long it took," she said.

The crowd finally accepted that and dispersed after much consternation. Finally, I confided that Grandma had told me her part of the secret about the jewelry.

"She did?" and appeared surprised for a moment before going into deep thought with her eyes closed and her hand over her mouth. Looking at me with her eyes half-closed, she said, "Well, I guess it's alright to explain a few things more that you may not have been told before. It can't hurt anyone now."

She told me that 'good old uncle' Harry, at the request of Mickey and others, had put Mrs. Gumm in protective custody at his home due to the information she had told him when he confronted her with Thelma's jewelry. After Reggie was killed and she, nor the jewelry, was needed at a trial, Mickey and Harry made sure she was given transportation to a destination of her choosing, so as to avoid any more harassment or bloodshed.

"To this day, I still don't know what became of her," she said. After giving her time to compose herself, she said, "Everything living, lives from the heart. Drunk or sober, sick or well, it's what's in your heart that counts."

I asked her what she thought was the key to having lived such a long and happy marriage and life. She said, "We always worked hard for everything we had. We never went to bed mad. We always discussed our issues and concerns in the morning. We didn't set around watching mindless game-shows or TV reality programs. We had enough reality of work that needed to be done surrounding us when we woke up each morning, let alone wanting to see more of it on TV. We never even had a TV until 1955."

"We ate what we raised on the farm, rich in fruits and vegetables, never taking out more on a plate than we needed to eat, and always eating what we took out on our plates. I never gave natural birth to a child, which can take an awful lot out of a woman and a man, like it did my mother and father. A spot to be born, a spot to die, and all the time between; that is all any of us have," she said.

"Who do you think was responsible for setting fire to the schoolhouse?" I asked.

"You have to understand, Rodger. In those days, people lived by the time-honored codes of conduct of the family and the clan they were part of. Now I wasn't there, and I don't know for sure, but the head of the family was responsible to, and for, all families and clan members.

"When a member of the family or clan was wronged, it was up to the head of the clan to insure the wrong was made right, by allowing those most wronged by injustice to prescribe the remedy and be given the opportunity to fill the prescription. When a person did wrong, it was up to the head of the family or clan to make things right by meting out justice for the wrong-doing. And if they didn't do so, a feud would start; family against family, clan against clan, and so forth," she added.

"That's how the Hatfields and McCoys, and countless other feuds, got started. Thank goodness we've come a long way since then," she quietly remarked. "The seeds of the good times we enjoy today were planted in the bad times of the past we endured and overcame. It wasn't about whom we were, or what we had become or evolved into, but rather what we had achieved and how we accomplished it that counted. Maybe it will have to be for each generation to learn the lessons of the past for themselves. Hopefully, they will learn from our mistakes and won't make the same ones we did," she said.

After several moments of silence with tears in her eyes and after blowing her nose, she said, "You know, Rodger, the souls of the innocent and forgiven will meet up yonder, come judgment day. I just hope yours' is there too."

I told her I planned on it and asked her if there was anything I could get her or do for her. She replied she had all she needed and I wished her many more happy birthdays. "Rejoice in every day," she said with two thumbs up, as she gave me a hug when I left.

Great Aunt Marie passed away in her sleep seven months later, just two months short of her 99th birthday due to congestive heart failure. She was buried with her husband, Gary, and I hope their souls are together in heaven, even if they didn't ask to be forgiven for whatever active or passive role they may have played in the 'shame of our county'. The minister, after the funeral, remarked again he had never known two 'sisters-in-law' who were as closely bonded as Aunt Marie and Grandma. They always seemed to end each conversation he had with them about the welfare of the other.

I didn't tell him why.

Most all the 'old' family in my life never lived more than twenty miles from where they were born. And when I die, I would like to be buried with them, even though I have lived my life in many places where my career has taken me. When I think of them hoeing weeds, shelling corn, hauling hay, and doing everything they could to scratch a living out of the land with their own bare hands, going shoulder to shoulder with sweat filling their eyes, working their guts out so the rest of us could have a chance to live, learn and prosper, I could just—

As the old saying goes, they weren't perfect, but they did the best they could with what they had.

Conclusions and Recommendations

In the final analysis, several conclusions about this episode in history can be noted. Firstly, while we search for appropriate remedies and focus on the things we have control over, that which can't be changed must be tolerated. And, trying to help without knowing how, can make a situation worse than it was, to begin with.

Seeing one's happiness slipping away can set the stage for a collective conscious dysphoria of the community-at-large, or an individual. Distorted, negative, irrational thinking errors were the basis for the actions that led to the demise of Thelma Holster and Reginald Gumm, who were both victims of the American social order of distant times.

Without disputing the negative, irrational thinking errors and beliefs that are common to people by virtue of just being human, and replacing them with more positive and constructive ways of looking at the world and ourselves, many unfortunate outcomes can result.

It seems obvious now, but judging a person by the group they are members of, or judging an entire group based upon the actions of one of its members, is an error in judgment based upon faulty reasoning and multiple thinking errors (e.g., global generalizations, 'mind reading', forecasting, etc.). Businesses, public or private, can trample a person's rights regardless of the consequences, without adequate safeguards for all people, workers or consumers alike. As a result, the most dangerous entity in any society is the person(s) who think(s) they have nothing to lose.

A child is the product of a union between a man and a woman, and the environment, physical and social, they were raised (inter-actionist model). The woman is the vessel of life, the first nurturer, teacher, and defender of the child, and the last to abandon them. In most societies, tradition has held that the man is expected to be the protector and provider of all, which is often too big a burden for some.

Both Thelma and Reggie were 'homegrown' products of the same county, and were seen by someone as necessary sacrifices for a mistaken 'greater good'. Thelma was hopeful and determined to pursue her career and seemed invincible in the face of everyday adversity but still naïve in the ways of the world, and ill-prepared to deal with the maniacal forces she would be confronted with, for whatever reason.

Reggie had so ingrained negative thinking and feelings after enduring a prison term, the loss of his wife, and daily struggles to provide for himself and family that he could rationalize just about any attempt to use his strengths to meet his needs, regardless of others' rights he might violate, and at the same time think he could get away with it.

Rushing to a judgment that is based on conjecture, myths, or rumors and not the facts, will not achieve justice for anyone and only appears to satisfy selfish revenge goals, whether it be for a group or individual. General talk is not based on definite knowledge, mere gossip or hearsay falls into two categories: Confirmed and unconfirmed. Both have to be substantiated, and only consistencies and contradictions within and between sources can lead to solid conclusions. Only an improved jurisprudence system that is allowed to proceed can accomplish that.

Professional labels for psychopathic personalities have been slow to catch up with those who have committed these two crimes; partly because most of us don't like to think that under the wrong circumstances, any of us could be just about capable of doing anything. Ultimately, we are all responsible/accountable for our own actions. We must all recognize the role we play in the issues and concerns that confront us, and resolve to work on the things we are capable of changing, while not spending our time trying to get control over the things we have no control over.

So, always get a perception check with someone in whom you have supreme confidence, and even double-check them too, if you think it is practical. The F.B.I. estimate, on average, there are 35 serial killers at-large in the U.S. on any given day, and some of those may not be

U.S. citizens. Therefore, don't take anything for granted when it comes to the investigation of crime.

And follow the law. If we are to insist on strict enforcement of the law, we must first do so by example. Without law, there is no civilization, or the opportunity to fully use our strengths to meet our needs in such a way that we don't infringe upon the rights of anyone else. I don't like the laws, work within the system of government to change them, but never take the law into your own hands. The law is for the protection of all the people.

Theories, old or new, must fit the facts, not twist the facts to fit theories, which is still a common problem in the minds of some people. They say 'never judge a book by its cover' because it is still a common mistake many people make, but has no room in modern scientific approaches to a analysis of human behavior.

People consciously, and/or unconsciously, tend to live up to the labels that have been stamped upon them, so much so, the label can become a self-fulfilling prophecy such as names, nick-names, diagnoses, prognoses, occupations, etc. Fallacies such as 'sickerts' are sickly, cancer equals a death sentence, and so forth, may keep us from seeing beyond and within the labels of life, and lead us to less intelligent decisions.

At the time of the murders of Thelma and Reggie, lynching/mob violence was defined as 3 or more persons acting in concert without the authority of law for the purpose of depriving any person of their life or doing them physical harm.

By this definition, I believe Alexander the Great, Julius Caesar, Abraham Lincoln, John Kennedy, and Lee Oswald, as well as many others, were 'lynched'. More currently it has been defined as to kill an accused person by mob action and without lawful trial, as by hanging, in defiance of legal local authority.

The term can be traced back in history to Capt. William Lynch (1742-1820), a member of a vigilance committee in Pittsylvania, Virginia, and has been credited with coining the 'Lynch Law' form of justice in 1780 for all those who defied the adopted laws of the government, based on the degree/severity of the crime they were accused of.

In those days, a person could be lynched for just about anything, depending upon their sex, ethnic, religious, racial, disability, social background, or affiliation(s). A hundred and fifty years later, things hadn't really changed much in Nowadays County. So, when you have a choice, never join an organization unless you know exactly what it's about.

I believe this episode represents the only time in our country's history a supposedly innocent victim was ritualistically 'lynched' by persons unknown to the general public. And on the same spot that at least one of the alleged perpetrators was subsequently 'lynched' with full public knowledge in such a way that no trace of either crime would remain intact enough for forensic examination with the exception of Thelma's body; both within 25 days of each other, as if swept away by the hand of God.

As for the future, more funding for research in forensic sciences should immediately be directed to institutions of higher learning and the U.S. Department of Justice/ Behavioral Sciences Unit of the F.B.I. They are greatly understaffed and under-budgeted for the task they have been assigned to apprehending the 'monsters among us'.

Instead of a ‘Top 10 Most Wanted List’, there should be a ‘Top 100 Most Wanted List’.

There needs to be an improvement in forensic guidelines to more quickly draw the attention of authorities to the victim and crime scene, and reduce crime scene and victim contamination, improve crime scene preservation, chain of evidence and evidence identification protocols, and zero tolerance for whoever divulges facts of a case before or after any kind of formal authorized investigation has begun.

Greater specificity in ‘modes of operation’ classification should be employed with computer technology advances. Analysis of dental and nasal scrapings retained by dentists or physicians and included in routine examination and autopsy procedures could reveal clues about events and individuals involved in activities of a criminal nature.

Increased awareness of perpetrator and victim characteristics and self-defense strategies should be taught in schools as part of basic survival techniques with ‘zero’ tolerance for bullying/teasing or stalking. The same guidelines used by car rental agencies for their customers should be learned by all citizens to increase awareness of potential dangers and what the best course of action would be for any circumstance involving compromised personal safety.

Improved video surveillance equipment on public and private vehicles, and in any areas known to have been the location of previous crimes could also be of benefit in confirming testimony and possibly eliminating or targeting suspects. If the tape doesn’t match the testimony, start probing for other inconsistencies and motives that can be useful in the solution to crimes.

Know where the nearest emergency services are available at all times and get there if you have the slightest hint that you have been targeted by a predator(s). It doesn't hurt to become acquainted with local authorities in advance, as well, so there is a record of concern if anything unfortunate should occur in the future.

We need to improve the way in which convicted criminals are evaluated for release back into society. The unusually high recidivism rates that have been reported by government officials suggest people are coming out of detention worse-off than they were before incarceration.

With psychological evaluations better tailored to the detection of aberrant value/belief systems and habilitation plans including continuing education/skill training opportunities, medical follow-up, counseling, and restitution in community/world service for the ex-offender, we can insist the individual 'repay their debts to society' and have a better chance of reducing the likelihood or re-offending.

In this manner, the guilty defendant could learn the social skills they never acquired in the first place, be more helpful than hurtful to others and have a better chance of being successful in work they can look at as a career and not just a job in the future. It would also be helpful to give the ex-offender a means of restoring full citizenship, where possible such as in the cases of 'white collar' crime or crimes not specifically involving violent acts toward others, as an added incentive for compliance with all the laws of our country.

Much of what I had always suspected about the story of Thelma and Reggie was never totally confirmed. Was Reggie guilty of the murder of Thelma? I believe so. If so, did he act alone, or were others involved? I believe others were involved. Could Reggie have simply been a pawn in a much larger plot? There's a good possibility of this.

What other forces might have had a hand in the deaths of Thelma and Reggie? At this point, it is impossible to know for sure without a complete forensic accounting audit of the entire county, and even that would most likely only reveal circumstantial evidence. As better methods of accounting and investigation are achieved, so are the chances of deterring crime.

And as hope may be the best of good things if remembered in the collective memory of the group or individual, no good thing ever completely dies. While it was lost in the minds of most of the people in Nowadays County alive at the time of this episode, hope never dies as long as we remember and learn from the errors of the past and resolve not to make the same mistakes again.

This story would forever cause doubt and wonder in everyone who heard or read about it. A mystery inside a headline, wrapped inside a myth, the story was immersed in secrecy, deception, fear, pride, and the passage of time. Unraveling what I could, took patience, effective listening, and persistence in pursuing the truth even when it eluded reason or was buried in a grave in Iowa.

Where does the collective conscience of society/civilization rest? In the grave with Thelma? Blown away with the ashes of Reggie? It never rests. It is continually evolving with the wisdom learned from successful experiences and never forgotten tragedies.

THE END OF 'SCHOOLHOUSE BURNING'

P.S.: I got an 'A' on my term paper and for the class.

Chapter III
Strengthening the Administration of Justice

Today in the United States, modern technology has made it possible to live longer and in greater numbers, to communicate instantly around the world, and to put people and multi-billion-dollar vehicles in space and under the seas for exploration and experimentation. Remarkable advances in the arts, letters, and numerous scientific disciplines have been achieved.

In the continuing evolution of a maturing democratic society, the United States has devised the best legal system in the world for resolving disputes and adjudicating people accused of a crime. Even so, the legal systems' complexity is not easily understood due to its many origins and historical influences. Several scholars have reviewed our legal system, and few have suggested alternatives that could improve it without violating the basic principle(s) of Western Jurist Prudence (McCart, 1964; Wrightsman, 1991; and Foley, 1993).

Though it may be unrealistic to expect it, this same system has not measurably deterred disputes or crime in most parts of society. The number of cases in our nation's court system has increased and decreased drastically over the last several decades with a litigation and 'rights' explosion, mass shootings, gang violence, child custody, etc., forcing some magistrates to be called away from their regular jurisdictions to try cases in others.

While some innocent defendants have been found guilty, some guilty defendants have gone free, and only a small fraction of the actual number of crimes committed each year ever come to trial (Foley, 1993).

While recognizing the increased pressures on the legal system, it has been only in relatively recent times that modern scientific advances have been applied to the work of our courts. Many states and federal jurisdictions still prohibit cameras, video equipment, or tape recorders in the courtroom (Kalven and Zeisel, 1971, Guinther and Walter, 1988). State Supreme Courts have vacillated between what would be allowed or not, with many appeals filed on behalf of 'right to know' interest groups.

Under increased pressures on the legal system, a decided lack of confidence in the courts has been noted after several controversial trials, including the cases of Rodney King, John Hinckley, Jr., the Menendez brothers, and others. Predicting a riot, perpetual appeals, and a continuing decline in public confidence in the courts could have been easily possible with whatever outcome was rendered in the California VS. O.J. Simpson trial.

The most sophisticated process ever devised for resolving conflicts and discovering the truth can lead to these reactions, apparently due to interactive effects of a 'circus-like' atmosphere surrounding the trial, the notoriety of the defendant, technical legal ploys, terms of the trial, and the prevailing sensibilities of the community-at-large regarding the nature of the crime.

Consequently, many citizens stand by helplessly, unable legally to do anything about a confusing, cumbersome, slow, and complex legal system that appears unable to meet today's advanced needs and demands, unless one is able to pay for 'high-powered' attorneys and trial consultants.

A Survey of Community Confidence

Every year for the past 10 years, in a face-to-face sidewalk interview survey, one hundred citizens (each year) of the U.S., over the age of 45, were asked, "Do you believe it is possible to get a fair trial in this country?"

Survey pool composition: 57% men and 43% women, with 89% being White and 11% being Black. No respondents were of Asian, Native American, or Hispanic descent. Of all respondents, 61% answered "No," 29% said "Yes," and 10% were undecided. When asked, "Why do you feel that way?" those answering "No," gave three general reasons.

First, 44% of those answering "No," said the laws are made to protect criminals. In fact, the rules for the courts are arranged so that it would be better for 99 guilty defendants to go free before one innocent defendant would be found guilty.

Second, 32% of those answering "No," said anyone opposing or taking issue with another person or entity can confuse a case with false testimony, unsubstantiated allegations, or nuisance cases; anyone can sue anyone for anything. This may be due to relatively few citizens getting caught and suffering dire consequences for impersonation, lying under oath, nuisance cases, and other forms of fraud and misconduct. The fluctuating prevalence of personality and mental disorders in society may account for a portion of these types of incidents.

Third, 24% of those answering "No" said the media's 'Blitz' of rehashing rumors or facts of a case before getting to trial can result in a 'trial by media' making it virtually impossible to find twelve unbiased impartial jurors not familiar with anything regarding the case. In some cases, courts have had to settle for jurors who have convinced the magistrate that they can maintain their impartiality, even though they admit to knowing or having heard about some aspect(s) of the case.

Those who answered "Yes" indicated two general reasons for their opinions. First, 53% of these citizens believed the people who had the responsibility of ensuring each trial is fair knew more about that area of expertise than the responder did. Second, 47% of these respondents who answered "Yes" had served on a jury or observed a jury trial, and felt it had appeared to be as fair as they knew possible at the time.

Of these, all admitted the most difficult part of their job as jurors were trying to remember what was said and what happened during the trial. Many felt frustrated due to being unable to ask some of their own questions at the time of a witness testifying. Jury duty appeared to be one of the hardest mentally challenging tasks they had ever undertaken and none wanted to do it again.

The 10% who indicated they were undecided had seen or knew of cases with similar complexity and circumstances that result in different verdicts, or where the courts treated people both fairly and unfairly without good reason(s) apparent to the respondent.

When asked, “What can be done to improve the legal system?” none of the respondents offered any constructive suggestions. Four percent of respondents spontaneously remarked, “The whole thing should be scrapped and start over.”

While some wanted to abolish the appeal process, return to corporal public punishment, or compulsory jury service, these could hardly be seen as constructive.

When notified of jury duty, most people try to find a way out of it, usually for self-satisfying reasons such as loss of wages, etc., forcing magistrates to take valuable time and money to look elsewhere for jurors. None of those surveyed were asked specifically if they had served on a jury, and none of the respondents were required to give their names or identification, though many did admit they had served and gave their names.

These results suggest a lack of confidence in the court system of this country and do not differ significantly from other recent surveys. If the undecided (10%) ever makes up their minds, even on an even split, the “Nos” could have a ‘super’ majority and call for a complete overhaul of the trial process while making life very difficult for every citizen.

A Baseline of Three Jury Trials

Baseline observations were made of three consecutive entire jury trials: Two criminal trials and one civil trial. Each trial lasted one day, as the magistrate had indicated it was his expectation at the beginning of each trial. Each trial included the voir dire (questioning and selection of prospective jurors), opening statements, questioning of witnesses/presentment of evidence, closing arguments, and jury deliberations. Each trial resulted in verdicts for the plaintiffs.

At no time were any jurors permitted to speak or take notes during the trials. In each trial, the magistrate read final instructions to the jury from a typed manuscript and provided it to the "Chair of the Jury" for the jurors' deliberations.

At the conclusion of the deliberations, the 'Jury Chair' returned the final instructions manuscript to the magistrate intact. In each trial, the counsels for the plaintiffs presented symbolic/graphic representations mounted on large cardboard/sheets and displayed on tripods in the form of maps, diagrams, and photographs of actual locations and crime scenes to illustrate their cases to the juries. Each was marked as court exhibits during the trials.

In each trial, all court personnel, magistrate, and attorneys were White and wore glasses, with the exception of the bailiff and the court stenographer, who were White but did not appear to wear glasses. In each criminal trial, the defendant was represented by a Public Defender, and no witnesses, other than the defendant in one trial, were called to testify for the defense. A total of twelve witnesses were called for the plaintiffs during the three trials.

A total of ninety-nine (99) perspective jurors composed the jury pools from which twelve-person juries were chosen; all being White, with an average age of 58.7 years. During the three trials, a total of four (4) jurors were observed to close their eyes with heads nodding for ten seconds or more on five separate occasions. One perspective juror got up and left the courtroom to go to the restroom, and one perspective juror told me he could get out of jury duty by telling the court he was a second cousin, twice removed, of the defendant.

There were no more than five private citizens in the public gallery of the court at any one time during the three trials after voir dire, with the exception of the final instructions stage in one criminal trial when five state witnesses also seated themselves in the public gallery. This researcher was seated alone in the public gallery for most of the three days while the trials were conducted after the voir dire process.

These baseline observations were undertaken at the suggestion of the local magistrate at the conclusion of a fifteen-minute conference held in his chambers. After an extensive literature and case review, two suggestions for improving the jury trial process (independent observer/monitor panels and videotaping the entire trial and replaying it if requested for jurors during their deliberations) were dismissed by the magistrate as flawed and contrary to current rules established by the Supreme Court.

When it was suggested to provide jurors with photographs of witnesses from the trial for their deliberations, the magistrate conceded he had never heard of that being done before and agree it did sound as if it might work as a 'memory jogger' device. Before concluding the meeting, the magistrate indicated he would check with a 'higher authority' before proceeding with a test case in the next scheduled jury trial.

In a previous out-of-state case, this same procedure had been tried. An appellate court ruled a witness photo would constitute an 'undue influence of a witness upon the jury and set the verdict aside'. These were the exact same words spoken to this researcher by the local magistrate in a private meeting at the conclusion of the baseline cases.

The strategy was revised to include photos of the judge, attorneys, witnesses and anyone so deemed appropriate by the court, so as to take into consideration the 'due' influence of all proper authorities for a balance of all influences upon the jury, and giving the judge authority to exclude any photo of anyone who was determined incompetent, immaterial, irrelevant and wholly without merit.

The local magistrate suggested contacting the Chief Justice of the State Supreme Court. A phone call was made with no success, as the Chief Justice was unavailable for comment, presumably involved in the first impeachment proceeding of an elected State Auditor. A letter was written outlining recommendations for improving the jury trial process. A reply by letter from the Chief Justice is included in the Bibliography/Supporting Resources section of this manuscript.

Dilemma for the Courts

Through many forensic laboratories around the world, and the Behavioral Science Unit of the Federal Bureau of Investigation, behavioral and physical science technology has been used to generate psychological profiles, numerous forensic investigative techniques and information for the apprehension and conviction of criminals (McCann, 1992, Blackburn, 1993, and Gamze, 1994). Defense counsels are claiming they need to be on 'even ground' with the government and are retaining their own experts in order to get a fair trial (Hambacher, 1994, and Weinstein, 1994).

Ultimately, the magistrate and jury are left on their own to sort through testimony and evidence more complex and detailed than ever before, such that it would take a person with near perfect memory to remember what happened and what was said, by whom, during the entire trial which could last for weeks, month, or even a day.

A Second Survey

In a face-to-face, sidewalk interview survey with one hundred twenty-eight citizens over the age of eighteen, I asked, "If you are picked as a juror in a trial, during your deliberations and in order to better remember what happened and what was said during the trial, do you believe it would be helpful to have a true and accurate photograph of each person speaking in any official capacity during the trial to include the judge, attorneys, witnesses and anyone so deemed appropriate by the court?"

This survey pool was made up of 64 women and 64 men. Of the respondents, 77 were White, 28 were Black, 14 were of Hispanic descent, and 9 were of Asian descent. All respondents signed and dated their opinions with the exception on one respondent who did not believe the photos would be helpful and refused to be interviewed further.

An overwhelming 90.6 % (116/128) of the respondents expressed that they felt the photos would be helpful, while 9.4 % (12/128) expressed the belief that photos would not be helpful.

Those opposing the use of photos were further interviewed and these citizens indicated they felt the photos would cause them confusion problems such as psychological disturbance, medical conditions, didn't understand the question, believed they already had a photographic memory, or failed to believe the court could ensure the security of the courtroom or the photos, which had nothing to do with the original question.

Discussion

Justice is swift and true in the courts of America. The dissatisfaction of the public with the courts noted above, turned on the legislative branch of the federal and many state governments, 11-8-94, when the U.S. elected the first Republican controlled Congress since 1954. It has also done so on a few occasions since.

Could the vast majority in this study be wrong? Do jurors have to look at the photos if they don't want to? Will people trying to mislead the courts think twice before they act when they know they are being photographed?

This researcher believes people will participate in trials more honestly when they know they are being photographed, and visual feedback devices such as still photographs can help a juror remember what was said and what happened in a trial, even when the trial is only one day long.

Whether it is by banks, places of employment, law enforcement officials, schools, etc., citizens are frequently confronted with requests for photographic identification throughout their daily lives to prevent abuses and apprehend wrongdoers in society. Credit and financial institutions are already converting to 'photo' credit and ATM cards for this same reason.

It is also noteworthy to consider another fact. Under the Sixth Amendment to the Constitution of the United States, accused citizens in criminal cases have the right to confront the witnesses against them, and this same right is generally extended to both sides in any trial by state constitutions. Implicit in the right to 'confront' is the assumption that people who say they are a given person, are, in fact, that person.

At this time, neither the defense, nor the plaintiff, nor the court requires 'real' positive photographic identification such as driver's licenses, passports, student I.D.'s, employment I.D.'s, etc., from trial participants during the trial, which can be independently certified and entered into a court exhibit record. States have been mandated to convert to 'real' identification systems by the end of 2020 or face consequences from federal authorities, but the uses of the identification devices still remain a question as to what will be allowed or not.

When a person stands up in open public court, swearing under oath to tell the truth, the whole truth and nothing but the truth, they hold out themselves and their testimony to the court to be self-evident that either a crime or transgression has been committed, or not, or the defendant or someone else has in some way had the means, motive or opportunity to have committed the crime/transgression, or not, expert testimony, or character reference for or against the defendant(s) or plaintiff(s).

Therefore, it only appears logical that true and accurate photographic identification of all trial participants deemed appropriate by the court could be admitted as a collective court exhibit. Each photo card, or actual photo obtained by the court if the participant didn't have one, could be properly displayed on a large cardboard sheet, in order of appearance and provided to the jury during their deliberations, if they so requested.

All photos and/or photo cards could easily be accounted for and protected by the sheriff or designee, and returned to the proper person at the conclusion of the jurors' deliberations, or sooner if so deemed appropriate by the court. While photos are not always the most flattering to the subject, one picture can be worth a thousand words when a juror is trying to remember what happened and what was said during the trial. (See the movie *Twelve Angry Men*)

Ideally, from an educational and leaning theory perspective, an audio-visual tape recording of the entire trial replayed for jurors during their deliberations, as needed, would help the collective memory of the jury better than still photos (Wrightsman, 1991). Unfortunately, such a tape could be manipulated or edited to falsify or take information out of context if not adequately protected.

A trial audit team such as a 'blue ribbon' panel appointed to independently determine the fairness of high-profile cases regardless of the guilt or innocence of the defendant could maintain the integrity of a jury trial. By using a written list of objective criteria, the audit team could observe the proceedings for the multitude of events that can occur to compromise the integrity of a trial.

Reporting any impropriety or misconduct to the proper authorities such as jurors falling asleep, prospective jurors leaving the courtroom without authorization during the proceedings, sexual harassment, racial prejudice, bias or discrimination of any kind, could be more easily noted for the basis of an appeal.

Such incidents can be overlooked by court personnel more involved in the specific tasks of their own individual work at the time, and can have a detrimental effect on a person's right to a fair trial. Such a panel would not be to second-guess the magistrate, but rather to admit our judges are only human with their own perspectives, orientations and perceptual abilities.

Additional strategies that could improve the trial process include:

1) Allowing jurors to silently write down questions for the magistrate to clarify any issue they may have at the conclusion of witness testimony, could result in an improvement of the juror's 'fact finder' role.
2) Because judges need to teach jurors about trial procedures, legal terms and concepts, etc.,

magistrates should be trained as teachers and be familiar with sound educational techniques, and thus be able to illustrate legal concepts with simple examples to facilitate the deliberation process.

3) To ensure magistrates and attorneys can see everything that is going on in the courtroom, they should be properly fitted with soft contact lenses, if and when they already need eyeglasses, to improve their vision. Contact lens wearers, who previously wore glasses, report improved visual acuity and peripheral vision. The importance of clear visual observations by everyone in a trial cannot be overstated.
4) Spoken instructions should be given at the rate of one word per second, or longer for more complex terms, for optimal learning and remembering what is said. (Note: this fact has long been known by the phone companies and psychologists/developers of short-term memory tests).
5) Each courtroom should be equipped with a fully visible, operational and accurately set clock for optimal time management requirements in conducting a trial, preferably on the wall behind the jury box, so as not to distract jurors.
6) At the conclusion of each trial, the magistrate should inform each litigant that they have the right to question the accuracy and completeness of their own criminal record in any and all databases for which a criminal record history is made (e.g., State Highway Patrol Criminal Records Division, Federal Bureau of Investigation, N.C.I.C., etc.).

> If an error is found, litigants have a right to bring suit for specific performance to correct the record and/or sue the designated authority for damages if the record is not corrected in a timely manner, or if the record is subsequently falsified in any manner.

Wrightsman (1991) also suggests the following reforms:

1) Seek to improve representativeness of the jury by severely restricting the types of people who are given exemption from jury duty and including people on driver's license lists, welfare rolls and city directories;

2) Reconsider the number of peremptory challenges awarded to each side and insist the judge ask the questions during the voir dire; and 3) videotape the trial presentation and edit it to remove objectionable material, then play it for the jury at the trial, and allow the jury to refer to it during deliberations.

Conclusions and Areas for Further Research

These recommendations would assist the jurors in remembering what happened and what was said during a trial, strengthen the position of all proper authorities in the trial process, reduce the incidents of perjury, nuisance cases and other forms of fraud and misconduct, and restore public confidence in our uniquely American Justice System.

As confidence in the judicial system of this country erodes, the incidence of lawlessness, bigotry, prejudice and class violence increase. After years of sociological research, we are finally at a point we must be willing to admit this and rethink how we can achieve a more fair and equitable system of resolving disputes/conflicts.

In the common law history of the jury trial, it was once believed the jury should be a jury of one's peers. In England during the negotiations over the Magna Carta with King John (brother of Richard, the Lion Heart), the English Barons insisted they be judged by a jury of their 'equals' to avoid deep resentments from 'lower' class groups and others that might overload or pack a jury pool for their own advantage.

Should we return to a definition of 'a trial by a jury of one's peers' as originally conceived in the Magna Carta? As racism appears to remain alive and well in the United States, as well as most other parts of the world, could it be possible to investigate whether all-black jury/court personnel should be used for white defendants and vice versa, and the same consideration for female vs. male defendants, etc.?

And to the contrary, would a white person be more or less likely to commit a crime if they knew they would be tried by an all 'black' or minority members court? And so forth for other demographic classifications such as old vs. young, disabled vs. non-disabled, etc.? Additional considerations for improving the justice system could result.

As a fair play, freedom and peace-loving democracy, we should be willing to help the collective memory of the aging jury pools of America to do their job as best they can. And, we should insist people officially participating in trials provide accurate photographic identification of themselves as proof that they are, in fact, who they claim to be. Only then will honest, decent and good people be less likely to find themselves at the mercy of the perjured, dishonest and guilty, tied up in a court of law or worse.

The true assets of our country are not in our material or technological treasures, but in the confidence of our people who have faith that our government is fair and equitable. When the confidence of the people erodes sufficiently, an act of misconduct can be expected to abound. While politicians point fingers blaming one another, and magistrates claim they don't make the laws, the people of this country can grow disillusioned.

If strategies for supporting our courts are not implemented, the very fabric of faith and confidence which hold our republic together could, in time, unravel under the pressures of increased social conflicts, intense scrutiny by 'right to know' interests, population explosions, technological advances and limited natural resources of our great democracy.

THE END OF 'STRENGTHENING THE ADMINISTRATION OF JUSTICE'

Chapter IV
The Republic of Jerusalem

Since people first came together in organized groups, many of their leaders have been possessed with the idea of world government and domination of all the known worlds' resources to serve their own self-interests and, in some cases, for the good of all.

Numerous forms of government have sprung up in virtually every part of the world attempting to achieve these ends. Dictators, fascists, communists/socialists, monarchs/royal families and even some forms of democracy have attempted to protect and expand their own way of life while only respecting the human and civil rights of some of the people under their rule in varying degrees. In some countries, select minorities have tried to force their will on their own and other countries with the aim of controlling the human and natural resources of their own country, as well as those of other countries.

Relative to the evolution of the earth, no government, including ancient Greek and Roman empires, has long endured or created a model for world government that would be responsive to, and meet, the needs of all the people it governed.

Since the signing of the Magna Carta, there has been a rise in democratic governments that have at least partially achieved the goal of meeting the needs of most of the people in the world while respecting the individual civil rights of all the governed. Just during the past century, attempts at democratic world government have come close to meeting and being responsive to the needs of all the people in the world (e.g., League of Nations, United Nations).

In both cases, they were established in the hope of avoiding world and regional conflicts, providing nations with a forum for resolving disputes peacefully, as well as assisting underdeveloped countries and those in need from natural and man-made disasters, as well as other humanitarian efforts.

It took two world wars to convince enough people that a democratic world government/forum could reduce the need for violence among the peoples of the world. It also could help those less fortunate countries address their priority needs for survival. Yet dissidents of virtually every kind continue to develop their networks of resistance and terror to promote their own self-interests and attempt to destroy all those who oppose them.

World Government/Forum Shortcomings

The United Nations is the latest less than entirely successful attempt at a democratic world government/ forum. This can be attributed to several reasons. First, there has been a lack of consistent support for the U.N. by all its members. Second, there has been an inconsistent response by the U.N. and the world's super-powers to terrorists and non-democratic governments that do not respect the human and civil rights of all people. And third, the seat of the world government/forum has not been located where most of the people in the world live; in the Eastern Hemisphere.

In total, this creates a perception of hypocrisy, alienation, uncaring/unresponsive attitudes and a lack of access to the seat of world government as a forum for all people. These were the same reasons the League of Nations, located in Switzerland, eventually failed after World War I.

Inconsistent support for the U.N. has been seen in many forms. This includes non-payment or late payment of dues, resolutions being ignored by dissident members, some members expressing ideal standards and expectation for all nations while they themselves have been unwilling to adhere too, etc.

Proven and unproven member state sponsored terrorism, theft and other forms of malfeasance and unethical conduct should also be considered as a lack of support for the goals of the U. N. For a more complete discussion, one need only talk to the Secretary General of the U.N. and these points become crystal clear.

Responses to terrorists and non-democratic nations have varied. Troop assaults only, bombing only, economic sanctions and embargoes with varying components, permitting some relief efforts while not others, limited recognition to full recognition with or without adherence to democratic principles, and many other unethical, unsanctioned or illegal approaches have had little success.

In the past, super-powers have even supported non-democratic governments and political assassinations of government rulers, officials and influential world citizens, rigging elections, breaking worker strikes, etc., when it served their interests. In many cases, the U.N. has been powerless to act and has not been timely when it did act, or acted inappropriately to the needs of the people in question.

For some parts of the world, this has been primarily due to the great distance from civilized areas and the lack of resources in some parts of the earth, as well as the unavailability of resources to the U.N. at the time.

The U.N. has long been viewed by many in the east as the 'puppet' of the West, intent on keeping the rest of the world under the control of 'Western Super-Powers'. Even while separated by two oceans, the U.N.'s founding fathers proclaimed the seat of world government/forum would be centrally located to all freedom-loving peoples, and in an area that could be secured from violent attacks.

This would supposedly permit everyone equal access to the world forum and the opportunity to speak freely, voicing their concerns without fear of retaliation. Given the fall of the 'Iron Curtain' and recent attempted and successful terrorist attacks, these have clearly been false assumptions.

A Case for the Republic of Jerusalem

Since the beginning of recorded history, and possibly before, countries whose seats of government were located where most of the governed were living would endure longer, regardless of the type of government they represented.

The more accessible the government was to most of the governed, and the more it protected the human and civil rights of all citizens in democratic formats, the more likely it would endure. Those governments that did not adhere to these principles would invariably fail due to internal and/or external factors that were unpredictable and/or uncontrollable for the governments in existence at the time.

Also, the world's most ancient travel/trade crossroads have met in what is now known as the Middle East. Jerusalem has been traditionally accepted as one of the Middle East's most ancient capitals and is virtually equal distance to South Africa as it is to China, or almost any other furthest points on the globe.

It has also been the flashpoint of conflict between many cultures of the world and the prize of many tyrants and religious groups, long before the Great Crusades, or the inception of Israel by the Super-Powers and the U.N., as a modern state. Due to its religious foundations as a Holy site for so many religions, it must be open to anyone who wishes to worship peacefully according to their religious beliefs without fear of intimidation or retaliation.

By moving the U.N., or at least establishing a new eastern capital of the U.N. in Jerusalem, or moving the current eastern capital of the U.N. to Jerusalem, all the world's people would be able to have equal access to, at least, a part of the world forum they have not enjoyed up to this point in time. A perpetual U.N. presence in Jerusalem could safeguard the rights of all people to worship at the Holy sights of their choice, as long as they abide by the laws of the Republic of Jerusalem and continue the missions/goals of the U.N. History has recorded the peaceful and necessary moving of capitals.

In the beginning of the most powerful nation on earth, the United States' capital was moved in order to be more equally accessible from north to south of the original thirteen states, being finally located in what is now present day Washington, D.C. The same experience for many of its individual states is noted as well.

In the case of this authors' home state of Missouri, the capital was moved from St. Louis in the furthest eastern part of the state to Jefferson City, which is about as far from Kansas City in the furthest western part of the state, as it is to St. Louis, and just about as far to the Iowa border in the north, as it is to the Arkansas border in the south.

By involving the world forum on a more permanent basis in the Middle East, it is possible to redistribute the world's 'political wealth' in favor of underdeveloped countries. Political stability would be achieved in the region with U.N. protection, while economic stability and prosperity for the region would follow. Western economists estimate between 60 to 70 million dollars (or more) are pumped into the economy of the U.S., particularly New York City, annually.

If this money were distributed to the citizens of Jerusalem, it could be a place of peace and prosperity, if also it is governed with its own registered citizenry, laws/constitution, elected officials and protected in perpetuity by all nations of the U.N.

In this manner, it can be open to anyone who wishes to come to visit or live according to the constitution and laws passed by the citizenry of the Republic of Jerusalem.

Consider these facts

May 14, 1948. David Ben-Gurion proclaimed establishment of Israel and was first to sign Israeli Declaration of Independence.

May 11, 1949. Israel admitted to the U.N. (37 in favor, 12 opposed, 9 abstained). Israel did not comply with U.N. resolutions calling for an international regime in Jerusalem, repatriation of Arab refugees and a need for a Palestinian homeland.

December 21, 1949. Israel moves its capital from Tel Aviv to Jerusalem and later back to Tel Aviv.

U.N. General Assembly Resolution 217 A (III): International Bill of Rights adopted by all nations except Saudi Arabia, South Africa and Soviet Bloc (finalization date undetermined/in dispute).

November 14, 1988: Chairman Arafat declares establishment of the State of Palestine at Palestine National Council Conference in Algiers.

November 15, 1988: Palestinian Liberation Organization voted 254 to 46 in favor of U.N. resolution 242 recognizing Israel's right to exist.

Goals

1. Establish the Republic of Jerusalem as an international city-state.
2. All freedom and peace-loving countries will consistently support the rule of law in member nations and support the implementation of consequences for violating international law through the World Court/International Tribunal and U.N./Security Council resolutions.
3. The U.N. will sponsor, monitor and certify open, free and democratic elections for any developing nation that doesn't have the resources to conduct

the elections themselves. Reward those countries having open, democratic and free elections, and who protect human/civil rights of all people. Consistently withhold rewards and/or punish those nations who do not abide by the will of the majority governed and the protection of the basic rights of all minorities as citizens of that nation.

4. All U.N. members will be role models in words and deeds, and advise all countries on the best possible actions to take in dealings with other nations on any matter of government and human relations.
5. Defend all people's rights to voice their opinions in the open forum of the U.N. and adhere to all countries' rights as member nations.
6. Relocate the Western or Eastern Capitals of the U.N. to the redefined (as necessary) city-state limits of the Republic of Jerusalem, or establish a new capital for the U.N. in Jerusalem, in addition to the two capitals of the U.N. already in existence. This area is more centrally located to where most of the people on the earth live, making the U.N. more equally accessible to all people in the world.

Israel can have its own capital in a town of their choosing, as can the Palestinians, while Jerusalem will be for all people of the world who wish to immigrate and live according to the laws of the Republic of Jerusalem. The U.N. Security Council can remain in New York City if it's determined by the U.N. to be in the world's best interests.

The majority of people who actually live in the original boundaries of Jerusalem are primarily of Arab/Palestinian decent.

In fact, Christian, Arab and Jewish people share a common heritage link that can be traced back thru antiquity by way of Moses and other prophets, all the way back to Abraham. If a free, open and democratic election in the native language of each person, 18 years of age or older in Jerusalem were held today, this author believes more actual inhabitants of this area could determine their own destiny more equitably than what has ever been achieved thus far in history.

For too long, foreign special interests have exerted undue influence on the people and natural resources of the Middle East, so much so, it seems to most people virtually impossible for the people of this area to feel they can determine their own destiny in a civil, peaceful and democratic manner.

By achieving the above goals, the people of this region could regain control over their own lives and resources, and assure a more prosperous outcome for generations to come, without the need for violence except in self-defense emergencies from non-democratic states/groups (e.g., criminals/terrorists, both foreign and domestic).

An ancient Greek philosopher once wrote, “I can’t fiddle, but I can make a great state from a little city.”

He was right. After all, whose child among us should be sacrificed for all the bricks and mortar in Jerusalem, or the Middle East, anymore? Is there a more proactive approach to resolving these conflicts and achieving world peace?

If not Jerusalem, then where? If not now, then when?

THE END OF 'THE REPUBLIC OF JERUSALEM'

Chapter V
A Case Study in Self-Hypnosis

What's Past Is Prologue

During the fall of 1997, I went back to school to obtain the then current course work requirements for a licensed professional counselor in the state of Missouri. I had obtained a master of science degree in counseling/ psychology, 1979, but at that time it was a 35 graduate hrs. program for which I already had 38 hrs. The requirements for L.P.C. were 45 hours in 1997.

After 18 years of Post-Masters experience in the field of professional counseling and psychology, which the Stare Board would not give me credit for, I found myself sitting in a graduate psychology class listening to a professor ask, "What is your happiest memory from childhood?"

I thought about it and came up with several experiences all occurring at the age of 5-7 years old. When I was told I could only choose one, I related the experience of watching a 4th of July fireworks display at the age of 5. Hand-in-hand with my mother and grandmother as we walked home after the display, I was so impressed I said, "This is the happiest day of my life!"

The instructor seemed to be making fun of my account, so I started to wonder, "OK. What should be the happiest memory of a person's life?"

After much introspective thought, surveying other students in class, friends and family members, I concluded being nursed by my mother and the taste of my mothers' breast-milk after my birth could be my happiest memory, or anyone else's for that matter. But 46 years after the fact, I couldn't immediately recall the taste of my 'first-feeding' experience.

I then remembered the theory of Hans Ebbinghaus (1885) I had studied in my first undergraduate class of General Experimental Psychology which suggested all events in a persons' life were stored in the persons' memory banks/cognitive systems. I also remembered the results of Joseph Breuer and Sigmund Freuds' *Studies on Hysteria* (1895), suggesting some mental illnesses were due to the repression of traumatic experiences of a persons' life in their unconscious mind.

In later works, hypnotherapy was suggested in the treatment of neuroses; recalling traumatic experiences to alleviate symptoms of mental illness, as well as achieving 'wellness through mindfulness' and increased awareness of one's own personal status. Consequently, it occurred to me that it might be possible through an age-regression approach in a deep relaxation/self-hypnosis format, to remember my first 'feeding' experience.

I would lay down in bed on my back, close my eyes and clear my mind of every thought; as a 'blank blackboard' for about 30 seconds. As I drifted into sleep, I asked myself one question, "What did my mother's breast-milk taste like?"

For about three weeks, during every waking moment I wasn't thinking about something else I needed to be doing, or when I went to sleep at night, or took a nap during the day, I would follow the same procedure, intently concentrate and ask myself this question, with no immediate recall of the experience coming to mind upon waking, or just during the day when daydreaming.

Finally, one Sunday afternoon after dinner at my grandmother's house, I took a nap alone in an upstairs bedroom. I decided I would give it the 'old college try' one more time and asked myself the same question as I slipped into a peaceful sleep. After about what seemed to me to be an hour of restful napping when I started to wake, I felt a tickling sensation in my lower right abdominal area that grew and expanded up my body to my throat, to my lower brain stem and upward through the middle of my head to its top.

The sensation then spread out all over the rest of my brain, much like a sensation of a liquid being slowly poured on the top of my head and dripping down the entire surface of my skull, only on the inside of it, and down through the rest of my body. It was like a warm water fountain erupting inside my head; a geyser of euphoria, with the entire process taking about 8-10 seconds; serious non-drug-induced pleasantness.

As the immense sense of pleasure began to subside, I sensed the taste of my mother's breast-milk on the tip of my tongue, so much so, I was aware that I was making slight 'sucking' motions with my mouth, licking my lips and sensed a distinct taste sensation that I could only relate to the experience I had when originally breastfed.

When I rose from the bed, fully alert with a slight dizziness, I had the most pleasurable sense of wellness I could recall in my life since my first 'feeding' experience. I ran downstairs and asked my grandmother if she had put anything special in the meal we had for lunch, or if we had any visitors that afternoon. She reported, "No," on both counts, and that I had actually been upstairs for about three hours. She thought I was doing my homework and didn't want to be disturbed.

Since then, I have been able to remember this initial 'out-of-the-womb' episode of my life with gradually less and less intensity/clarity, but with remnants of the original experience always there in my memory. I have found all subsequent events to it, neutral, positive or negative, were much more easily recalled, understood, accommodated and accepted in a more realistic and healthy perspective.

Also, I seem to have occasional simple random memories of events of no major significance from just about every stage of my life that seem to just spontaneously 'pop into my head' from time to time with no adverse effects and, in some cases, being very insightful and instructive.

Call it a hypnopompic gustatory hallucination, overactive imagination, self-stimulation of glandular hormone release(s), or what you will. I have been unable to find anyone who can report having had any similar 'recollection' event. In fact, I've heard leading experts in the field of 'memory' say it was impossible for a sane person to have had such an experience, or bring any memory of their lives prior to the age of 5 years to conscious awareness (Stuart Zola, Ph.D., 4/16/99, verbal report).

I'm the eldest of five children, and have never spent a day of my life as a patient in a hospital, except once when I was born and once when I had my tonsils and adenoids removed at age 10. I have had most of the usual ailments/conditions of childhood: measles, mumps, etc., which all resolved with proper medical attention.

I have never taken any routine medications with the exception of an aspirin for periodic 'cold/flu'-like symptoms (maybe 6-8 per year). I have never had any broken bones, while I did sprain my left ankle at age 14, and my right shoulder at age 21, which both healed without complications. I've also been lucky enough to never have had what experts would call a particularly 'traumatic event' in my life, or any sign/symptoms of mental illness.

Since acknowledged experts were so skeptical, I've been reluctant to suggest this procedure be used by anyone else. Unfortunately, a situation has arisen that has made me feel it would be less intrusive than many current methods addressing the 'wellness' needs of people.

Thus, after completing a 15-year follow-up study on the procedure with myself and finding no adverse side-effects which could be attributed to the procedure, I embarked on an investigation to determine its efficacy in promoting wellness in others.

Introduction

Throughout the history of mankind, people have marveled and wondered with awe at the human minds' capacity to remember the past with varying degrees of clarity, insight and 'self-defensiveness'. Attempts to explain the most complex phenomena on earth have filled countless volumes on psychology and human development with many astounding conclusions being achieved for the betterment of mankind. And yet, many questions are unanswered and remain areas for further research, particularly in regard to repressed memory and the development of personality, developmental and clinical syndromes/disorders of psychopathology.

It has long been argued that the foundation of mental health is physical health. But it has also been argued that conditions of mental health have been the cause of physical health issues. While the mind/body dualism argument preoccupied the forefront of psychotherapy over the past two centuries, holistic, cognitive-behavioral and nurture/nature interactionist models appear to have won the day, with 'wellness through mindfulness' approaches gaining much popularity, at least in theory.

The results of initial investigations are encouraging, if also lacking the rigor adhering to the foundations of behavioral science research.

The question still remains as to exactly how a person overcomes the trial and tribulations of life without the display of signs/symptoms of mental illness. Do we just believe that by distracting ourselves with thoughts that are incompatible with the feelings of emotional or physical pain, we can alleviate the negative feelings or physical illnesses?

Or, as in the past, by putting ourselves in the hands of magicians or trained professionals, they will make everything all better just by waving some magic wand, passing their hands over us, or just by venting our feelings to a proper person in the proper place at the proper time, can improve our psychological condition with little or no effort on our part? Will taking pills or having surgical operations help a person learn emotional or behavioral control? Can believing in 'will and determination' lead to overcoming any obstacle?

If just hoping things will turn out 'OK' were enough, we wouldn't have the rising tide of depression, suicide, substance use/addictions disorders and behavioral/mental health issues confronting us today, as have been reported by just about every world, national, regional and local health authority in existence.

Where does hope for the alleviation of emotional and physical pain (e.g., trauma-resolving experience) and the belief in a brighter future come from? Freud said to look deep within your 'self' to recall the traumas of your life and come to a new appreciation for their meaning and resolution(s). He didn't report going back as far as birth trauma of a person's life in his practice of psychoanalysis. But he and his colleagues appear to have been on the right track.

Some might consider it impertinent to think someone, somewhere, hasn't already tried to recall their first 'trauma-resolving' event by use of self-hypnotherapy/deep relaxation techniques. We habituate to the experience early in life, so much so, it is beyond taking for granted and is continued with cow's milk for most of the rest of our lives. It is the first crisis of life that must be resolved successfully if we are to survive.

The trauma of birth may not be all that traumatic for some, while very much so for others. It may include use of forceps or cesarean procedures, and circumcision in the case of live male births. The first natural crisis of natal and postnatal life can overshadow prenatal trauma, as well.

It is the position of this author that hope comes from the conscious, subconscious or unconscious memory of the first 'trauma-resolving' event (e.g., any event that alleviates physical and/or psychological pain) in an infants' life. Their first-feeding experience, preferably with their biological mother's breast-milk that is genetically matched to the nerve receptors of the infant which coats the nervous system and resolves birth trauma, fulfills this role if all other things are equal for adequate warmth, safety and proper environmental stimulation.

This is also assuming that both parents are healthy, both physically and mentally, without infections, toxic levels of pathogens, free of prenatal, natal, and postnatal injuries, or genetically predisposing factors in developmental disabilities.

Literature Review

An extensive review of the professional literature in the history of psychology and psychotherapy, from both Eastern and Western civilizations, has failed to reveal any mention of suggesting an individual could, should or would attempt to remember the taste of their mothers' breast-milk, or any other first-feeding experience, so as to gain a new appreciation for their entire life span experiences, including all traumas subsequent to birth (Rosenfeld, 2008; Hergenhahn, 2001; Wetzenhoffer, 2000; Lynn and Rhue, 1991).

The evolving definition of terms used to explain the models of human memory and mental functions has reflected modern research to a great extent while also retaining some of the origins of the terms. To begin with, most of the terms were based on ancient Greek myths such as Phobia (the earliest arch-type), Eros, etc. Hypnosis is Greek for sleep and James Baird (1843) is credited with deriving the term hypnosis from the then medical models' neurohypnology: the study of nervous sleep.

Today, the American Psychiatric Association defines hypnosis as a state of decreased general awareness with heightened attention to a constricted or localized area of stimulation, such as repetitive suggestions by another person involving consciousness, memory, anesthesia or paralysis.

The state usually is associated with the feeling that the subject is behaving non-volitionally even though aware of what the behavior is. Factors determining the subjects' responsiveness include the nature of the pre-existing relationship with the therapist/hypnotist, prior expectations, beliefs and motivations concerning hypnosis and most important, character and individual differences.

By contrast, the American Psychological Association defines hypnosis as the procedure, or the state induced by that procedure, whereby a hypnotist suggests that ta subject experience various changes in sensation, perception, cognition, emotion or control over motor behavior. Subjects appear to be receptive, to varying degrees, to suggestions to act, feel and behave differently than in a normal waking state.

The exact nature of the psychological state, uses and effectiveness of hypnotic procedures as therapy remain the subject of much debate and on-going research. Self-induced hypnosis (autohypnosis) may occur spontaneously or be achieved through training in auto-suggestion. Hypnotic regression is defined as a technique of hypnotherapy in which an individual under hypnosis is induced to relive a past experience that has been forgotten or inhibited but may be contributing to an emotional conflict (VandenBos, 2007).

'Conscious', according to the American Psychiatric Association, is defined as the content of the mind or mental functioning of which one is aware, while 'unconscious' is defined as that part of memory and mental functioning that is rarely subject to awareness. It is a repository for data that have never been conscious (primary repression) or that may have been conscious and are latter repressed (secondary repression).

According to the American Psychological Association, in classic psychoanalytic theory, conscious is defined as the region of the psyche that contains thoughts, feelings, perceptions and other aspects of mental life currently present in awareness. The content of the conscious is thus inherently transitory and continuously changing.

Consciousness is defined as the phenomena that hums report experiencing, including mental contents ranging from sensory and somatic perception to mental images, reportable ideas, inner speech, intentions to act, recalled memories, semantics, dreams, hallucinations, emotional feelings, 'fringe feelings' (sense of knowing) and aspects of cognitive and motor control.

Accordingly, an 'altered state of consciousness' is a state of psychological functioning that is significantly different from ordinary states of consciousness. It is characterized by altered levels of self-awareness, effect, reality testing, orientation to time and place, wakefulness, responsiveness to external stimuli, memory ability, or by a sense of ecstasy, boundlessness, or unity with the universe.

'Subconscious' is considered by some as an obsolete term that was formerly used to include pre-conscious (what can be recalled with effort) and the unconscious. 'Pre-conscious' is the level of the psyche that contains thoughts, feelings and impulses not presently in awareness but which can be more or less readily called into consciousness such as the face of a friend, a verbal cliché or the memory of a recent event (fore-conscious).

Unconscious, in psychoanalytic theory, is the region of the psyche that contains memories, emotional conflicts, wishes, and reported impulses that are not directly accessible to awareness but have dynamic effects on thought and behavior, marked by the absence of awareness or lack of consciousness.

By contrast, the American Psychological Association defines memory as the ability to retain information or a representation of past experience, based on the mental processes of learning or encoding, retention across some interval of time, and retrieval or reactivation of the memory, specific information, and past experiences that are recalled; the hypothesized part of the brain where traces of information and past experiences are stored (memory storage, memory system).

Along with further research in memory, several new terms such as associative memory, auditory memory, constructive memory, implicit and explicit memory, long-term memory, and immediate (short-term) memory have been formulated.

In the evolution of psychology, it should also be noted there has been much dissension in the ranks of other professionals defining terms in the study of the mind. Schacter (1996) defined hypnosis as a social process in which the suggestion and cues provided by the hypnotist, guide the hypnotized individual through an imaginative role-playing activity, and hypnosis does nothing to enhance the accuracy of memory retrieval.

It was contended hypnosis creates a retrieval environment to increase a person's willingness to call just about any mental experience a 'memory' with no reliable way to tell the difference between accurate memories and illusory ones. Illusory memories were frequently noted in highly hypnotizable people, even when no formal hypnotic induction was used. Social pressure can affect memories of events that never occurred and yet hypnotized people do occasionally recall actual experiences they might not otherwise remember.

Eventually, the American Psychological Association, Division 30-The Society for Psychological Hypnosis, defined hypnosis as usually involving an introduction to the procedure during which the hypnotized is informed cues for imaginative experiences will be presented.

The hypnotic induction is an extended initial suggestion for using one's imagination and may contain further elaborations of the introduction. The procedure is used to encourage and evaluate responses to suggestions. When using hypnosis, the subject is guided by the hypnotist to respond to suggestions for changes in subjective experience, alterations in perception, sensation, emotion, thought, or behavior.

Most people can also learn self-hypnosis, which is the act of administering hypnotic procedures on one's own. If the subject responds to hypnotic cues, it is generally inferred that hypnosis has been induced. Many believe that hypnotic responses and experiences are characteristic of a hypnotic state. While some believe it is not necessary to use the word 'hypnosis' as part of the hypnotic induction, others view it as necessary (American Psychological Association, 2005).

Joseph Breuer (1842-1925), a mentor to Sigmund Freud and who Freud credited with being the father of psychoanalysis, hypothesized that when the memory of a traumatic event is recalled under deep relaxation of hypnosis, there is a release of emotional energy (catharsis) and the symptoms caused by the repression of the negative memory are relieved (Breuer and Freud, 1895).

At the time, they didn't explain fully how this occurred but suffice it to say, their focus was on the traumatic event and left it to the individual to explain the phenomena for themselves and recognize the covert and overt behaviors suggesting mental illness resulting from repressed memories as being erroneous, irrational, or self-defeating and of no worthwhile use.

Freud (1915) would later explain his theory of mental illness with the use of numerous hypothetical constructs, many of which still remain in the professional jargon of psychiatrists, psychologists, and other mental health professionals today. This is not to say he failed to recognize there were many obstacles to curing mental illness, as many of his patients would substitute other symptoms when the initial symptoms were extinguished, or described memories of events that could not be confirmed as actually having happened.

Also, he discontinued the use of hypnosis when he discovered many patients were possibly feigning hypnotic states and didn't want to disappoint their famous therapist; eagerly complying with his suggestions (Freud, 1917).

While numerous followers of Freud put their own interpretation of his work with observations and techniques of their own, they all continued to focus on the retrieval of negative memories from traumatic events as the best way to address underlying causes of mental illness. Many contributions were made to expanding this same model, addressing this same phenomenon from the perspective of independent objective observer to dependent subjective interpreter, and many perspectives in between (Forrest, 1999; Mitchell, 1995; Gibson and Heap, 1991; Linden, 1990; Lawrence and Perry, 1988; Rowley, 1986; Hilgard, 1970; Hilgard, 1965; Horney, 1942; Hull, 1933).

Based strongly on the medical model of diagnosis followed by treatment, the psychoanalytic and Neo-Freudian movements were not without its critics, and those who wished to consider additional implications for accenting the 'positive'. With much debate as to exactly how the brain functions from a generalized functioning perspective of the brain as a whole, versus a localization of functions perspective, higher cortical functions still remain very much a mystery (Gaylin, 2001; Pinker, 1997; Kirsh and Lynn, 1995; Loftus and Ketcham, 1994).

Strict Freudian, Neo-Freudian, neuro-behavioral, humanistic/client-centered, and holistic perspectives are still argued as the best approach to take in promoting the further positive growth and development of people, as well as the psychotherapy of mental illness, with genetic and developmental perspectives having their own contributions and criticisms of everyone else, as well (Stern, 1985; Benson and Klipper, 1976; Spitz, 1965).

A reasonable person would wonder why they all aren't talking to one another as at the Ebbinghaus Centennial Conference (Hoffman et al., 1986).

Otto Rank (1924) theorized that birth trauma was the most significant factor in determining future personality development. Rank, nor his followers, suggested the 'birth trauma-resolving' event should be a primary focus of attention in psychotherapy, or how to build upon this event so as to assist in the adaptive resolution of subsequent traumatic events. Just finding 'a good story' in a person's life, as suggested by Gaylin (2001), does not appear to be enough. Remembering the 'best one' might.

A Single-Subject Case Study

Directive Hypothesis: When the memory of an individuals' 'first-feeding' experience alleviating the psychological and physical pain of birth (e.g., 'birth trauma-resolving event') is recalled under an altered state of consciousness, as the person passes into a conscious, alert state, there is an internal release of emotional and/or physical energy-producing substance(s) allowing the individual to re-experience the sensation of their 'first-feeding' experience.

This is confirmed by independently observing the 'suckling' and tip of the tongue 'licking lips' behaviors of the individual and the subjects' subsequent verbal self-report of the event. Then, over time, the symptoms resulting from the repression of negative memories are relieved through the recall, understanding, accommodation, and acceptance of the traumatic events that followed the actual 'first-feeding' event.

Case Subject (S): a 41 year, 5 months old Caucasian male, approximately 72 inches tall, weighing 190 lbs., fully ambulatory, with brown hair, brown eyes, and no distinguishing scars, tattoos, or allergies. He is the second of five children born to his biological parents and reports he thinks he was told by his mother that he was breastfed until about age eleven months with no known serious medical, mental health, or developmental issues noted in his history.

He is college educated with a Bachelor in Business Administration/economics degree and works as a claims adjustor for a nationwide insurance company. He has been married for the past 20 years and is the father of one daughter, age 16, and one son, age 15. His wife is 39 years of age and a healthy 'stay-at-home' mom. He was solicited as an unpaid volunteer for an experimental investigation in 'self-age-regression' and, after signing the necessary release, confidentiality/privacy, and service agreement forms, he requested to remain anonymous.

Method: The subject was seen for his annual physical examination within 30 days prior to the start of four one-hour weekly individual office visit sessions. The medical examination did not reveal any medical problems.

In the first session, S was administered a standard psycho-diagnostic clinical interview with a mental status exam. No signs or symptoms of mental illness or personality disorders were noted, and S was lucid in conversation and well-oriented to general and specific limits of time, place, person, purpose, and danger reality referents in his surroundings with average to above average intelligence noted. He was courteous at all times and responded to courtesy appropriately.

He easily established trust and indicated he had recently been having mild-to-moderate difficulty getting to sleep at night but did not feel comfortable taking sleep-aide medication. S was instructed in self-hypnosis with standard induction procedures (Copeland, 1995) simply to relax and enjoy a restful sleep and was given several relaxation tapes he could choose to listen to on his own, in the privacy of his own surroundings.

At the conclusion of the first session, he was given the following instructions: "Each time you go to sleep at night, take a nap during the day, or just when you are not busy with other activities you need to be doing, I would like you to use the relaxation procedures we discussed and retrace your life back to the first time you were breastfed by your mother, recalling the taste of your mother's breast-milk upon waking.

"Give yourself a visual image of holding a lit candle while standing atop a large spiral staircase that becomes gradually narrower as you step down each step into the darkness below. Each step you take down the staircase represents a year of your life in reverse order until you reach the last step, representing the first year of your life. As you are about to touch the bottom, you will be at the point of having had your first-feeding experience."

He was seen for three more individual sessions, each one a week apart, over the next three weeks, to discuss how he had been sleeping, areas of stress (improving coping skills), life in general, and if he had at any time recalled his 'first-feeding' experience.

Results: At the second session, S stated he had been sleeping much better and seemed to be getting more work done; accomplishing tasks he had been procrastinating about over the past several months, but he had not had any recollection event of his 'first-feeding' experience. We discussed how he was doing in his relationships with his family and co-workers, which all seemed to be unremarkable. He related he did not quite understand why I had asked him to try to remember such a distant event in his life, but was willing to continue trying with as much concentration as he could focus on the topic.

At the third session, S stated he had continued to rest well at night and seemed to take fewer naps during his off hours during the week. We discussed his plans for the future and his general satisfaction with his life, which was good, but still no recollection of his 'first-feeding' experience. He admitted he had not always remembered to think about his assignment each time he went to sleep or when 'daydreaming', but promised he would try to do better over the coming days.

At the fourth session, S stated he had continued to rest well with the exception of two days when he experienced ‘cold/flu-like’ symptoms which resolved with aspirin therapy by the morning of the third day, (two tablets every four hours, as needed, for two days). He stated he had enjoyed our sessions and felt he had gained a great benefit from them, and was considering pursuing an M.B.A. degree, which would allow him to advance his career and help pay for his children’s college education.

He stated he had still not had any recollection of his ‘first-feeding’ experience but would continue to try to remember it in the future. I thanked him for his honesty and cooperation with the experiment and asked him to let me know if I could be of any further service to him or his family.

Ten days later, when I got to the office, S had left a message stating he had recalled the taste of his mother’s breast-milk upon waking that morning. I immediately called him and asked him what it had been like in more detail. He stated he had become a little restless upon waking and noticed he was making ‘suckling motions with his lips, slight ‘cooing’ sounds, and licking his lips with his tongue just before rising fully alert in his bed’.

He stated he was so amazed, he thought he was in ‘heaven on earth’. He became slightly frightened and was about to call an ambulance when he sprang to the side of his bed and started laughing so gleefully as the intensity of the experience began to subside. He didn’t know what to think.

At that point, he called and left his message. He stated he didn’t think he could have had such an experience in the presence of another person. His wife and children had gone to his in-laws for the weekend and he was working at home on his computer most of the time they were gone.

"It was too intimate, personal, sensual, vulnerable, beautiful, and wonderful, all at the same time; like wanting to laugh and cry for joy all at once. It was like a fountain of youth erupting inside my head and spreading throughout the rest of my body!" he said joyously.

Also, he stated he had just happened to remember his assignment when he went to sleep, and decided he would try to remember the taste of his mother's breast-milk in a less focused manner; "Come what may."

I told him I would be doing 30-day, 6-month, and one-year follow-up studies to see how he was doing, which he agreed to. Each subsequent visit suggested he was well and had no signs of adverse side-effects. At the one-year follow-up visit, S reported he was near completion of his M.B.A. degree and his daughter had been accepted at a local college majoring in nursing.

His wife was also planning to go back to school and work part-time while his son was finishing high school. S wanted to know when he was going to be able to tell his friends and family about his experience. I stated we would have to wait until the study was finalized and additional research was completed before suggesting the procedure be used with others on a large scale.

He reluctantly agreed and confided he had originally 'down-played' the reason he had volunteered for the experimental investigation to begin with. He stated in retrospect, he was much more anxious and concerned about how he was going to pay for his children's education than he had told me at the beginning of the experiment but was feeling much better about it now.

Discussion

This study suggests that while it is true the first predictable reaction to a primary or secondary negative stimulus/experience is pain and/or shock, to move beyond that status hypothetically requires an internal release of substances that re-coat the affected nerve receptors and alleviates the physical and/or emotional pain reaction. This study suggests it is possible to recall 'trauma-resolving' events, even as far back as the first one that provided sustenance for life out of the womb and began to resolve birth trauma.

This study also suggests the experience of resolving birth trauma may be the first event that gives an individual hope for a promising future while going on with the finding of resolutions to all the conflicts of life; unconsciously holding its memory 'on the tip of one's tongue,' so to speak. 'Lip service' to the conscious memory of the happiest experience from your childhood is a good start at finding a 'happy story' in a person's life, but it should be followed by the recall of the first 'trauma-resolving' event and all subsequent events over the person's life span at the discretion of the client.

It appears the use of self-hypnosis, meditation, deep relaxation, and sleep, when focused on the reliving of 'trauma-resolving' events, can have a positive effect on the mental status of people and could be used before more invasive, intrusive, or possibly dangerous procedures are employed to alleviate some conditions of mental illness.

This study is limited in that it only studied one person; sometimes called a 'one shot case study' who was given the suggestion (stimulus) to retrace his life back to near his beginning and recall the taste of his mother's breast-milk.

The subject was not confined to laboratory settings or administered any invasive procedures. Only the Diagnostic Interview was utilized as a measure of mental wellness and did not suggest the subject was suffering any distress at the beginning or end of the experiment.

Only the verbal self-report of the subject and direct observations of the subject were taken as prima fascia evidence of the procedure's effects. Kerlinger (1975, 2nd Ed., pages 314-26) further examines the shortcomings of single-subject research designs in terms of the generalizability, reliability, and validity of such studies. This study is taxonomic with the intent to discover/document previously unreported natural phenomena of human nature.

In the immortal words of Vernon and Jeffery Mark (1992): "—don't become impatient with yourself when the retrieval process takes longer than you'd like. If you have a large memory bank with a substantial catalog of memories, don't expect all of them to pop to the surface without some effort on your part to concentrate and make the memories you need (want) available" (p.17).

Conclusions and Further Research

Much remains to be learned about the human psyche and the ability of a person to recall their first trauma-resolving/breast-feeding event which appears to have been discounted or overlooked throughout the history of mankind. The potential benefits of this procedure in promoting wellness in people need to be further investigated.

Long-term randomized, double-blind controlled studies with more complete medical examinations, numerous laboratory studies (CBC, platelets, etc.), psychological evaluations, and psycho-social histories are needed to determine if, in fact, this procedure can have the desired effect in relieving symptoms of mental illness on large groups, or subgroups of clinical populations.

Obtaining baselines of beta, alpha, and theta EEG% differences, serotonin, beta-endorphins, norepinephrine, cholinesterase levels, and various dependent variables of immune function and positive effects on self-awareness/acceptance, to compare with post-intervention findings, could reveal more specific effects of the procedure. Whether or not this procedure can be reliably used to promote 'wellness through mindfulness' in the human experience, remains to be more fully determined.

Also, the genetic basis of hypnosis susceptibility should be further researched to determine specific parameters of such a unique human phenomenon. It may or may not be normally distributed across the human species.

Happiness is not the absence of trauma; to live is to suffer. For some, traumatic events may not have been satisfactorily resolved and it is one of the therapists' jobs to assist the individual with the successful adaptive resolution of those events that continue to haunt the human mind.

When a person starts to lose hope and confidence in themselves and their futures, the first question they ask themselves is, "How in the world did I ever get to this point in my life?"

The answer to this question is best discovered by starting at the beginning of that life, so as to be able to retrace one's steps up to any point in that life, past or present. Therefore, the essence of human happiness could be the satisfaction that comes from the conscious memory and knowledge of that person's 'trauma-resolving' events in their life.

Whether there is a given destiny for each of us, or if we are all just floating like flowers on a great sea of time, accidentally stumbling into the future, or a combination of both, look deep within the center of your 'self' in your own time and space to discover what you've forgotten. Then, with the memory and knowledge of the resolution of past traumas, put the past into perspective so you can get on with your future.

A person's memory is like a deep sea of secrets, myths and truths, only a small portion of which are revealed to the conscious mind until they are unlocked by the 'will' of that person.

THE END OF 'A CASE STUDY IN SELF-HYPNOSIS'

Bibliography and Supporting Resources

American Psychiatric Association: Diagnostic and Statistical Manual of Mental Disorders, 5th ed., (DSM-5). Washington, D.C.: American Psychiatric Association, 2013.

American Psychological Association (2005) 'A New Definition: Hypnosis', Div.30, *Society of Psychological Hypnosis.* (http:/www.apa.org/division30/define_hypnosis.htnnl)

Andreasen, N.C. and Black, D.W. (eds) (2001 and subsequent edition) *Introductory Textbook of Psychiatry*, 3rd Ed. Washington, D.C.: American Psychiatric Publishing.

Barlow, D.H., Tranel, D., and Anderson, S.W. (2009) *Abnormal Psychology: An Integrative Approach*, 5th Ed. Belmont, CA: Wadsworth Cengage Learning.

Benson, H., and Kilipper, M.Z. (1976) *The Relaxation Response*, London: Hogarth Press.

Blackburn, R., *The Psychology of Criminal Conduct: Theory, Research and Practice*, Chester, England: John Wiley and Sons.

Blair, J., Mitchell, D., and Blair, K. (2005) *The Psychopath: Emotions and the Brain. Malden*, MA.: Blackwell Publishing.

Braid, J. (1843) *Neurypnology or the Rationale of Nervous Sleep Considered in Relation with Animal Magnetism*, Buffalo, N.Y.: John Churchill.

Breuer, J. and Freud, S. (1955) *Studies on Hysteria* in the Standard Edition (Vol. 2), London: Hogarth Press.

Christensen, L.O. (1999) *Dictionary of Missouri Biography*, Columbia, M.O.: University of Missouri Press, p. 359-60.

Cooper, M. (1986) *Life, Liberty and the Pursuit of Happiness in Nodaway County, Missouri, a Black History, 1840-1940*, Maryville, M.O.: Northwest Missouri State University, p. 279-85.

Copeland, R. (1995) *How to Hypnotize Yourself and Others*, N.Y.: F. Fell Publishing, (2nd Ed).

Deupe, R.A., and Lenzenweger, M.F. (2005) A neurobehavioral dimensional model of personality disturbance. In M.F. Lenzenwerger and J.F. Clarkin (Eds.),

Major Theories of Personality Disorders (pp. 391-453). N.Y.: Guilford.

Dobbert, D.L. (2007) *Understanding Personality Disorders: An Introduction,* Westport, CT.: Greenwood Publishing Group Inc.

Ebbinghaus, H. (1964) *Memory: A Contribution to Experimental Psychology* (1885) in H.A, Reger and C.E. Bussenius, Trans. N.Y.: Dover.

Foley, L.A. (1993) *A Psychological View of the Legal System*, Dubuque, IA.: Brown and Benchmark/Wm. C. Brown.

Forrest, D. (1999) *Hypnotism: A History* (Previous Title: The Evolution of Hypnotism), London: Penguin Books.

Frazier, H.C. (2009) *Lynchings in Missouri, 1803-1981*, Jefferson, N.C.: McFarland and Co.

Freud, S. (1955) *A Difficulty in the Path of Psychoanalysis (1917)* in J. Starchy (Ed. and Trans.), the Standard Edition, Vol. 17, pp. 136-44, London: Hogarth Press.

Freud, S. (1966) Introductory Lectures on Psychoanalysis, (1915-17) in J. Starch, Ed. and Trans, N.Y.: Norton.

Gabbard, G.O. (2000) *Psychodynamic Psychiatry in Clinical Practice*, 3rd Ed, Washington, D.C.: American Psychiatric Press.

Gamze, J.C. (1994) *Forensic Psychiatry: The Interface Between Neuropsychology and Forensic Issues*, Springfield, IL.: Charles C. Thomas.

Gaylin, W. (2001) *How Psychotherapy Really Works: How It Works When It Works and Why Sometimes It Doesn't*, N.Y.: Contemporary Books/McGraw-Hill.

Gibson, H.B. and Heap, M. (1991) *Hypnosis in Therapy*, London: Hogarth Press.

Guinther, J. and Walther, B. (1988) *The Jury in America, and the Civil Juror: A research Project Sponsored by the Roscoe Pound Foundation*, N.Y.: Facts on File Publishing.

Gunderson, J.G. (2001) *Borderline Personality Disorder: A Clinical Guide*, Washington, D.C.: American Psychiatric Publishing.

Hales, R.E. and Yudofsky, S.C. (eds.) (2003) *The American Psychiatric Press Textbook of Clinical Psychiatry*, 4th Edition, Washington, D.C.: American Psychiatric Publishing.

Hambacher, W.O. (1994) 'Expert Witnessing: Guidelines and practical suggestions', *American Journal of Forensic Psychology*, 12 (2), pp.17-35.

Hare, R.D. (1993) *Without Conscience: The disturbing world of the psychopaths among us*, N.Y.: Pocket Books.

Hergenhahn, B.R. (2001) *An Introduction to the History of Psychology*, 4th Ed. Belmont, CA: Wadsworth/Thomson Learning.

Hilgard, E.R. (1965) *Hypnotic Susceptibility*, N.Y.: Norton.

Hilgard, E.R. and Hilgard, J.R. (1975) *Hypnosis in the Relief of Pain*, Los Altos, CA.: Kaugman.

Hilgard, J.R. (1970) *Personality and Hypnosis: A Study of Imaginative Involvement*, Chicago, IL.: University of Chicago Press.

Hoffman, R.R., Bringham, W., Bamberg, M. and Klein, R. (1986) Some Historical Observations on Ebbinghaus. In D. Gorfein and R. Hoffman (eds.), Memory and Learning: The Ebbinghaus Centennial Conference. Hillsdale, N.J.: Erlbaum.

Horney, K. (1968) *Self-Analysis* (Original work published 1942), N.Y.: Norton.

Hull, C.L. (1933) *Hypnosis and Suggestibility: An Experimental Approach*, N.Y.: Appleton-Century.

Innes, B. (2005) *Body in Question, Exploring the Cutting Edge of Forensic Science*, N.Y.: Sterling Publishing Company.

Intrator, J., Hare, R., Strizke, P., Brichtswein, K. Dorfman, D., Harper, T., et al. (1997) 'A Brain Imaging (Single

Photon Emission Computerized Tomography) Study of Semantic and Affective Processing in Psychopathy', *Biological Psychiatry*, 42, pp. 96-103.

Kalven, H. and Zeisel, H. (1971) *The American Jury*, Chicago, IL.: University of Chicago Press.

Kaplan, G.B., Hammer, R.P., Jr. (2002) *Brain Circuitry and Signaling in Psychiatry: Basic Science and Clinical Implications*, Washington, D.C.: American Psychiatric Publishing.

Kerlinger, F.N. (1973) *Foundations of Behavioral Research,* 2nd Ed., N.Y.: Holt, Rinehart, Winston, Inc., pp. 314-26.

Kirsh, I. and Lyn, S.J. (1995) 'The Altered State of Hypnosis: Changes in the Theoretical Landscape'. *American Psychologist*, 50, pp. 846-58.

Lawrence, J. and Perry, C. (1988) *Hypnosis, Will and Memory*, N.Y.: Norton.

Linden, W. (1990) *Autogenic Training*, London: Penguin.

Loftus, E. and Ketchan, K. (1994) *The Myth of Repressed Memory: False Memories and Allegations of Sexual Abuse*, N.Y.: St. Martins' Press.

Lynn, S.J. and Rhue, J.W. (ed.) (1991) *Theories of Hypnosis*, N.Y.: Norton.

Mark, V.H. and Mark, J.P. (1992) *Reversing Memory Lose: Proven Methods for Regaining, Strengthening and Preserving Your Memory*, N.Y.: Houghton, Mifflin.

McCann, J.T. (1992, Fall) 'Criminal Personality Profiling in the Investigation of Violent Crime: Recent Advances and Future Direction', *Behavioral Sciences and the Law*, 10(4), pp. 475-81.

McCart, S.W. (1964) *Trial by Jury: A Complete Guide to the Jury System*, Philadelphia: Chilton Books.

Millon, T. (2004) *Personality Disorders in Modern Life*, N.Y.: Wiley.

Miller, N. and Dollard, J. (1939) *Social Learning and Imitation*, New Haven: Yale University Press.

Mitchell, S.A. (1995) *Freud and Beyond: A History of Modern Psychoanalytic Thought*, N.Y.: Basic Books.

Pinker, S. (1997) *How the Mind Works*, N.Y.: Norton.

Rank, O. (1929) *Das Trauma Der Geburt* (The Trauma of Birth), 1924, English Trans. N.Y: Basic Books.

Raper, A.F. The Tragedy of Lynching. Chapel Hill, N.C., 1933. Reprinted N.Y.: Dover Pub., 1970.

Rosenfeld, S.N. (2008) *A Critical History of Hypnotism: The Unauthorized Story. Cincinnati*, OH.: XLIBRIS, Corp. (Ships from, and sold by Amazon.Com)

Rowley, D.T. (1986) *Hypnosis and Hypnotherapy*, London: Penguin.

Schacter, L. (1996) *Searching for Memory: The Brain, the Mind, and the Past,* N.Y.: Basic Books.

Shahrokh, N.C. and Hales, R.E. (Eds.) (2003) *American Psychiatric Glossary* (8th Ed.), Washington, D.C.: American Psychiatric Publishing, Inc.

Sisson, N. (1911) *The Illustrated Historical Atlas of Nodaway County*, Missouri. Chicago, IL.: Anderson Pub. Co., Sec. 2, p.1.

Spitz, R. (1965) *The First Year of Life*, N.Y.: Basic Books.

Stern, D.N. (1985) *The Interpersonal World of the Infant: A View From Psychoanalysis and Developmental Psychology*, N.Y.: Basic Books.

Vanderbos, G.R. (Ed.) (2007) *American Psychological Association Dictionary of Psychology*, Washington, D.C.: American Psychological Association.

Webster's New World Dictionary, Encyclopedic Edition. New York, N.Y.: The World Publishing Co., 2010.

Weinstein, J. (1994) *Expert Hired by Simpson Team to Help Pick Jurors*, Los Angeles Times, p.3.

Wrightsman, L.S. (1991) *Psychology and the Legal System*, Pacific Grove, CA.: Brooks/Cole Publishing Co.

Yudofsky, S.C. and Hales, R.E. (eds.) (2002) *The American Psychiatric Press Textbook of Neuropsychiatry and Clinical Neurosciences*, 4th Ed., Washington, D.C.: American Psychiatric Press, Inc.

Yudofsky, S.C. (2005) *Fatal Flaws: Navigating Destructive Relationships with People with Disorders of Personality and Character,* Washington, D.C.: American Psychiatric Publishing, Inc.

Zimmerman, M., Rothschild, L. and Chelminski, I. (2005) *The Prevalence of DSM-IV Personality Disorders in Psychiatric Outpatients*, American Journal of Psychiatry, 162, pp. 1911-18.

Recommended Websites

www.behavioraltech.com
www.borderlinedisorders.com
www.borderlinepersonalitydisorder.com
www.bpdcentral.com
www.mclean.harvard.edu/research/clinicalunit/psychosocial.php
www.menningerclinic.com
www.schematherapy.com

About the Author

Rodger B. Moore is a single white male, divorced/widower, with no children. He is a retired counselor with a Masters in Counseling Psychology and over 40 years of post-Masters experience in the mental health field and human support services. He recently semi-retired due to increased demand for services. He enjoys hiking, chess, swimming, and dancing. He does not consume alcohol or tobacco. He has a 'have plan, will travel' attitude and is an ideas-driven person with a 'helping' orientation. He expanded his practice to include mediation services. He has never been convicted of a felony, is up-to-date on all vaccinations, has never been sued for malpractice, and has never lost a client to suicide.

Dedication

This book is dedicated to Reva McDonald.